THE CATS' FAMILY TREE

A journey into history by
Miss Mac

Miss Mac lives at the church of St Hubert in the tiny village of Dunsop Bridge in the beautiful surroundings of Lancashire's Forest of Bowland, together with her companion, Ko-Ko. Ably assisted by the Parish Priest of St Hubert's, Fr John Chaloner, they have published these other titles:

Miss Mac the Church Cat, an Autobiography

Ko-Ko the Church Cat Who Found Love

Both are available from Redemptorist Publications.

THE CATS' FAMILY TREE

A journey into history by

Miss Mac

patiently scribed by

JOHN CHALONER

A Redemptorist Publication

Published by **Redemptorist Publications**
A Registered Charity limited by guarantee.
Registered in England 3261721.

Copyright © 2009 John Chaloner

Text and Illustrations: John Chaloner
Layout: Rosemarie Pink

First published in 2009

ISBN 978-85231-363-3

All rights reserved. No part of this publication may be reproduced, stored in a retrieval system, or transmitted in any form or by any means, electronic, mechanical, photocopying, recording or otherwise, without prior permission in writing from Redemptorist Publications.

The moral right of John Chaloner to be identified as the author of this work has been asserted in accordance with the Copyright, Designs and Patents Act 1988.

A CIP catalogue record for this book is available from the British Library.

Printed by Lithgo Press Limited, Leicester LE8 6NU

Redemptorist
PUBLICATIONS
Alphonsus House Chawton Hampshire GU34 3HQ
Telephone 01420 88222   Fax 01420 88805
rp@rpbooks.co.uk   www.rpbooks.co.uk

Contents

Introduction
Roots   7

Chapter One
Friendship by Lady MacCavity of Iou Island   25

Chapter Two
Courage by Cogitosus of Lindisfarne   49

Chapter Three
Wisdom by Mythanwy of Cwm Pennant   77

Chapter Four
Kindness by Macushla of Gleann Da Loch   99

Chapter Five
Perseverance by Cocco of Greccio   123

"But now it's 'Good morning, Goldilocks' and 'How are you, Goldilocks?' and all because you want something."

Introduction

Roots

I had seen the priest standing on the small wall that runs alongside the road. He seemed to be looking for something. Eventually he climbed down from the wall and opened the big door of the church.

"Ah, there you are, Mac!" he exclaimed. "I was looking for you. When did you come into church? Surely you haven't been in here all the time?"

The Cats' Family Tree

Of course I had. This sort of question is so typical of the priest. He hadn't noticed that I had been asleep underneath a pew near to the organ. No one had noticed me. Few people ever do, unless I choose to sleep near to the altar. Then they notice me. "Oh, look," they whisper. "There's a cat. Is it real?" And sometimes, just to show them that I am real, I jump onto the altar and have a wash.

One night I was asleep near the altar when I was disturbed by a resident bat flying around aimlessly. I followed him with my eyes and in so doing my attention was drawn to the paintings that adorn the ceiling above the altar. I think the priest calls it the apse, but why he doesn't just say ceiling I don't know. Here are images of a horse, a bull, a dog and a deer, an assortment of angels and below them an eagle, an ox, a lamb and – strange to tell – a lion. I sat spellbound as I gazed at these images when all at once I heard a voice.

"Do you know your roots?" It was the horse.

"Roots? What do you mean – roots?" I asked.

"Do you know where you come from? Do you know who your ancestors were? This sort of thing is all the rage nowadays, you know."

Roots

"I haven't the faintest idea," I replied. "I know that I was abandoned when I was a kitten, and that the priest rescued me and brought me here. Other than that, I know nothing at all."

"That's very sad," said the horse. "We should all know at least something about our roots."

"But," I added, "I do know my name. The priest gave me my name when he appointed me Church Cat. I'm Miss MacCavity, or Miss Mac."

"I'm Kettledrum," replied the horse. "I won the Derby in 1861. I brought in quite a tidy sum of money, I can tell you. Indeed, it's said that my winnings helped to pay for the building of this little church of Saint Hubert, Dunsop Bridge. That's why I'm here in the apse, you know."

"How verrrry impressive," I said.

Kettledrum gently snorted in agreement. "But tell me," he continued, "who are your parents? You can trace your family roots through your parents. At least, it's a start."

"I don't even know that," I replied despondently. "I don't know who or where they are. Do you know about your parents?"

The Cats' Family Tree

"Oh yes. In fact I can trace back my lineage for some considerable way. I know that I was born in 1858, that my father was Rataplan, my mother was Hybla, that her father was Provost, her mother was Otsini, and that Otsini's father was Liverpool. I might add that all of these horses were thoroughbreds to the nth degree."

"That's all very interesting," said another voice. "But you should remember that some of us in this apse can trace our ancestry back much further than that."

"Who are you?" I asked.

"I am Egremont and I'm an eagle. Actually, I'm here in the apse as a symbol of Saint John the Evangelist. His Gospel is known for the depth of its theological vision, and eagles, as everyone knows, have vision that is second to none."

"I've never met an eagle before," I replied. "Are you a local?"

"Hardly," he said, rather disdainfully. "We eagles prefer the higher peaks north of here but generally we keep our distance and appear only rarely." He gave me a piercing look and added, "Usually when we see something we'd like to eat."

Roots

I thought it best to keep the conversation going and so I asked hurriedly, "How far back can you trace your ancestry?"

"Oh, right back to biblical times," he replied imperiously. "Indeed, our importance in the scriptures cannot be overstated." He then added, even more imperiously and with what I suspected was a liberal touch of sarcasm, "I don't expect you will recall – despite your frequent attendance in church – that God delivered the Israelites from slavery and brought them to Mount Sinai?"

"As a matter of fact, I do. That was where God spoke to Moses on the mountain and gave him the Ten Commandments, was it not?"

The Cats' Family Tree

"Good heavens! You amaze me. I never thought for one moment that a cat would know anything about the scriptures. You have obviously listened attentively to the priest's sermons."

"We cats always listen, no matter how onerous the circumstances. We hear things that no one else can hear."

Again he assumed his air of superiority. "Well, then, in that case you will, no doubt, have heard that when God conversed with Moses on Mount Sinai, God was said to have 'carried his people on eagle's wings'? Or of how Moses sang of God's love for the people and compared it to an eagle that watches its nest, hovers over its young, spreads out its wings to hold them and supports them on its pinions?"

"Yes indeed," I replied. "I believe that your first example was from the Book of Exodus and the second from Deuteronomy."

"You amaze me even more," he said, but now with a rather subdued voice.

"I'm sure I do. You see, I am very well acquainted with the scriptures and this is because of my frequent conversations with Goldilocks, the marble angel in

Roots

the church cemetery, not to mention the discourses in which I engage with Saint Hubert himself whose image, as you know, is in the stained glass window at the west end of the church."

"Oh well, in that case there is nothing more to be said," he responded gloomily, his superior air having been totally deflated.

"You could have added", I suggested, relishing this unexpected turn of events, "that 'the way of an eagle through the skies' is one of the four things that even a wise man cannot comprehend. You will find that quotation in the Book of Proverbs, of course."

"Of course," he replied – and said no more.

"This is all very well," said another voice from the apse. It belonged to the lion. "All of us can trace back our ancestry by using such generalisations, but generalisations are often quite meaningless."

"What is your name?" I asked.

"I'm Leonidas and I represent Saint Mark."

"Why?"

The Cats' Family Tree

"To be honest, I'm not absolutely sure," he replied. "But probably it's because we lions have a tendency to roar and it is said that Saint Mark's Gospel evokes a similar image when in the opening lines he speaks of a voice crying in the wilderness."

"What an intriguing comparison," I observed. "The more so since you and I belong to the cat family, do we not?"

"Well, yes in a way I suppose we do, but…" There was a long pause and then he said, "I don't quite know how to put this, and I certainly don't mean to be unkind, but this is precisely my problem with generalisations. It is true that we belong to the cat family, but domestic cats are much smaller than lions and don't roar as lions do, so I can't help but feel that any affinity between us is rather tenuous, to say the least. Oh dear, I haven't offended you by saying this, have I?"

"Of course not," I said, perhaps a trifle unconvincingly. "But you've obviously never heard me growl, or hiss. I can be quite fearsome when I growl or hiss."

"I've heard you growl and hiss," said another voice. It belonged to the ox.

"When was that?" I asked.

Roots

"When the priest tried to lift you from the altar after you jumped onto it while he was saying Mass," he replied.

"I didn't mean any harm," I said. "It's just that I like to be involved in whatever is happening."

"Yes, I've noticed," said the ox. "You also jump onto the window ledges and it's not unknown for you to climb onto the altar reredos."

"The what?" I asked in surprise.

"The carved screen behind the altar. I have often seen you walking along the upper ledge of it, there between the carvings of horse heads, you seem to use it as a short cut when the priest is saying Mass."

"Could I ask your name?" I enquired (mainly to change the subject). "And could you tell me if you also represent a saint?"

"My name is Oxymoron," he replied. "The saint I represent is Saint Luke and before you ask why, I shall tell you. Oxen are beasts of burden and Saint Luke's Gospel gives hope and joy to all who are burdened in any way."

"How comforting," I replied.

The Cats' Family Tree

Leonidas now brought the conversation to a halt. "Comforting it may be," he said, "but only Kettledrum here knows precisely who his ancestors were and I think we should now draw a line under the whole thing. I, for one, am going back to sleep."

"So am I," said Oxymoron.

"I might as well do the same," said Egremont. "Let's all go back to sleep."

"Nay," said Kettledrum (a word frequently used by horses). "We can't leave such an interesting matter suspended in mid-air."

But they had all gone back to sleep.

"Well, really!" Kettledrum exclaimed. "How very inconsiderate of them."

"It doesn't matter," I said.

"Of course it matters," responded Kettledrum. "It's important that you should know about your family tree."

At that moment, Ko-Ko, the Associate Church Cat of Saint Hubert's, ambled into the church. He saw me, but totally ignored me, and continued down the aisle to the back of the church. Ko-Ko jumped up onto the basin

Roots

which contains holy water – the stoup, I've heard the priest call it, but we prefer to regard it as a drinking bowl. Ko-Ko drank, then he jumped down, ambled back along the aisle, sat near the altar and had a wash.

"Hello, Ko-Ko," I said. "Do you know anything about your roots?"

"My what?" he replied while vigorously licking his front right paw.

"Your roots. Your family tree. Where you come from. Who your parents are; who your grandparents, great-grandparents, ancestors were."

"No idea at all," he replied as he began to wash his front left paw. "All I know," he said in between licks, "is that I came to Dunsop Bridge from Tosside in Yorkshire when I was a kitten and that when I was left alone and looking for food and somewhere to sleep the priest came to rescue me." After saying which, he commenced washing his back right leg.

"Well, *I* would certainly like to know about *my* family tree," I said, wistfully.

Ko-Ko said nothing but after a while began washing

The Cats' Family Tree

his back left leg. When he had done that he turned his attention to washing his tail. Next he washed behind his left ear; then he washed behind his right ear. When everything had been completed to his satisfaction, he gave a very big yawn, stretched out his front paws, sat down again, turned to me and said, "As you well know, when we cats wash, we don't just wash, we also ponder. Well, I have been pondering."

"Pondering about what?" I asked.

"Your question about my roots, of course," he replied, "and I have come to the conclusion that it would be a good idea if you and I together try to discover our ancestors."

"Well pondered!" exclaimed Kettledrum. "Then what I suggest is that you both have a word with Goldilocks the angel. She has many connections in high places."

And so that is what we did. The next morning, Ko-Ko and I trotted into the cemetery after breakfast. I jumped onto the plinth beneath Goldilocks' feet while Ko-Ko sat near to one of the graves and, as you might expect, began to wash himself.

"Good morning, Goldilocks," I purred. "How are you? We are here to ask you a question."

Roots

"Yes, I thought as much," she replied – somewhat ungraciously. "I cannot help but notice how on some days you and Ko-Ko spend hours mooching around the cemetery or in the wood across the road and totally ignore me, but now it's 'Good morning, Goldilocks' and 'How are you, Goldilocks?' and all because you want something."

"We don't mean to ignore you," I replied. "It's just that we're preoccupied with other things."

"If I may say so, that is a rather feeble excuse and on a par with the kind offered by people who forget to say their prayers until they want a favour from God," responded Goldilocks. "However," she continued, "be that as it may. What is this question of yours?"

"Well, I was going to ask you how we could discover our family tree."

"What a decidedly odd request. I have always been under the impression that the cat family has no particular tree. On the contrary, if a tree is there, you, and all the other cats that have lived here, simply climb it – with no questions asked. You all seem to assume that *every* tree is your own."

The Cats' Family Tree

"We don't mean that kind of tree," I replied. "We mean our family history. We are trying to discover our roots."

"Roots, indeed! Why are your 'roots', as you call them, so important to you?"

"We would like to know who our ancestors were," I said. "Kettledrum knows such a lot about his family. Egremont the eagle is very proud of his ancestry – even though he can give no specific details – but we would be happy with just a few stories. As you are an angel, we wondered if you might have access to such information."

"How very perceptive of you," she replied. "We angels are indeed in a very privileged position, living, as we do, in celestial bliss – except, that is, when we are down here guarding family vaults as I do. Now I think about it," she continued, "I could possibly ask my angelic colleagues to help."

"Oh, would you?" Ko-Ko said, excitedly. "That is so very kind."

"Not at all," she said, pleased that she was being given something to do other than meditating in the church cemetery. "I shall have a word with the angelic archivists. I know them all very well, of course. They are known as 'Recording Angels' and are kept extremely busy. They have to record everything that goes on in the world. But they have a most efficient filing system, far better, indeed, than any earthly computer system. Nothing is missed and no mistakes are made through human error, as the people in heaven are barred from interfering in their work. It is an extremely satisfactory state of affairs."

What a good idea it was to give Goldilocks something to do! Giving others something to do ranks high in the list of a cat's priorities. Take, as an example, the relationship that Ko-Ko and I have with the priest who lives with us. If he is in the garden and we want him to take us for a walk, all we do is sit by the gate leading to the path along the side of the beck. This is a sign to the priest that he is to open the gate and let us through. Of course, we could just as easily crawl underneath the fence – but why should we when the priest is at hand? It gives him something to do. The same principle applies whenever we are all together in the house and Ko-Ko or I wish to go out. We simply sit at the front door. Of course, the priest knows that we can just as easily go out through the cat flap in the back door if we want to. What is more, he knows that we know we can use this other form of exit but he always obliges by opening the front door.

The Cats' Family Tree

Naturally, the process of achieving this response from the priest has demanded much patience on our part, but then we cats are experts in the virtue of patience. I find that, as a general rule, if one perseveres with humans — and, indeed, with angels — they invariably come round to our way of thinking.

By now, having been given something to do, Goldilocks was positively brimming with enthusiasm. "Who knows what the heavenly archivists will find?" she said. "It's all very exciting. Come back tomorrow as I may well have something for you."

And so the next day we returned to the cemetery. Goldilocks and the Recording Angels had exceeded every expectation. Not one, but a number of records had been discovered.

"The fascinating thing about these records", Goldilocks noted, "is that all your ancestors were Church Cats. Curiously, they all enlisted the help of the priests or the monks or nuns who lived with them to pen their memoirs. What is more, each one lived in places that were, or were to become, centres of pilgrimage."

"How verrrry gratifying," I said as we purred with contentment.

Roots

Over the months that followed, I have dictated to our priest all the information given to Goldilocks by the Recording Angels. And so you may share our investigation into our feline ancestry with the first of these memoirs, previously available only to the heavenly archivists.

"I cannot stress too strongly that this is MacCavity land."

Chapter One

Friendship
by Lady MacCavity of Iou Island

There was a storm out at sea and the rain was lashing along the shore of the island. Having sheltered in a cavity under some white marble rocks, I was warm, dry and totally untroubled. This should come as no surprise to anyone. You see, I am a cat and all cats are wise. Our wisdom always guides us, no matter how inclement the weather, to find the snuggest and most comfortable place in which to bed down and sleep. Although I say it myself, I am extremely

The Cats' Family Tree

competent in finding these hiding places, especially cavities under the rocks. Probably this is the key to the origin of my name. If I explain that I am a Scots cat you will understand more readily. As you will know, many Scots prefix their names with "Mac" and it therefore follows quite logically, bearing in mind my proclivity for finding cavities, that I am "MacCavity", a name which, roughly translated, means "Clan of the Cavities". Indeed, my full title is "Lady MacCavity of that Ilk".

But allow me to continue my story. There I was, warm and snug, when through the rain and the mist something made me sit up with a start. It was a boat battling against the storm and slowly but surely making its way to the shore. On board there was a lot going on: men dressed in long garments were attempting to gain safe passage to the shore. But what drew my attention most of all was a small figure sitting at the stern. I looked hard and – yes, without any doubt whatsoever, it was a cat.

The boat came into shallow water; the men on board climbed over the sides, and began pulling it onto the shingle. As soon as it was secured, others jumped overboard. But (as is the custom of our species) the cat waited and weighed up everything carefully before attempting to jump. The opportunity was seized when

Friendship

two men staggered by under the weight of a large wooden cross. Then, with great accuracy, the cat leaped onto the cross and secured safe passage to dry land.

My first reaction was one of total dismay at this unwarranted invasion of my territory. I growled, and growled again. In fact I kept on growling until the men and the cat moved into the distance and disappeared over a hill. Then and only then did I realise that there was only one course of action open to me: I went back to sleep.

It was a good and deep sleep, which probably lasted some hours, before I awoke again. By now the green and white pebbles on the shore glistened in the sunlight and the arch of a distant rainbow joined earth to heaven. I decided to have a wash. Of course, we cats regard washing as a most serious business, so serious that we do not welcome interruptions. But interrupted I was – by a small voice.

"Miaow."

It was the boat cat.

Every sinew in my body tightened. The natural instinct to defend my territory voiced itself again in a growl, this time a long continuous growl. The intruder likewise

The Cats' Family Tree

growled. Then we sat facing each other in silent confrontation for a long time – a very long time indeed – and neither of us took our eyes off the other, or allowed our bodies to relax, even momentarily. The silence grew in intensity until finally I squealed at the intruder, "Don't you know that you are invading MacCavity land? Who are you and what are you doing here?"

"I am Colcu," the intruder squealed back.

"You still haven't told me why you are here!" I screeched.

"I don't know why I'm here!" he screeched back. "All I know is that I've been brought to this island by Abbot Colum Cille and his monks from Ireland. I didn't ask to come, did I?" And he gave a long growl.

"Why did you come here?" I squealed.

"I keep telling you! I don't know!" he squealed back.

Again there was a long silence. No longer did we squeal or screech. We glowered and glowered. Indeed, we glowered so much that now the silence was deafened with our hostility. Perhaps this state of affairs would have gone on and on, had not Colcu been the first to make a move towards friendship.

Friendship

"We have got off to a bad start," he said, "and I'm sorry that I have upset you. I don't even know what island this is."

"You are on Iou, or the Island of the Yew Trees, and I cannot stress too strongly that this is MacCavity land. But you are a stranger here and I should have welcomed you. Let us make the best of it."

"I'm willing to do that," Colcu replied. "Abbot Colum Cille says that it is good to welcome the stranger."

And in this way we became friends. Indeed, we became the very best of friends. After some time I joined Colcu in a little dwelling of timber, wattle and turf where one of the monks lived with him and over the next few months Colcu and I were busily engaged in overseeing the monastery's building programme. At set times during their work the monks would stand still, sit or kneel down and chant prayers together. Quite often we would join them in their prayers and when we did so, if we could find a sitting monk with a convenient and vacant lap, each of us would nestle down and go to sleep.

One day our slumbers were rather rudely disturbed. A tall, long-necked bird had suddenly appeared. It was pacing up and down a large piece of timber that lay on the ground.

The Cats' Family Tree

"Good heavens," cried one of the monks. "It's Abbot Colum Cille's pet crane! He must have followed us from Ireland." He and the others rushed off to find the abbot, leaving Colcu and me alone with the crane.

Now you will understand that we cats don't normally converse with cranes (or any other birds for that matter) but this time curiosity got the better of me.

"Hello," I said. "Who are you?"

"I'm Cronan Grus-Grus," he replied.

"That's a remarkably long name," I said.

"Yes, it is rather," he agreed. "But it is one of which I am extremely proud. It shows my pedigree, you see. It is double-barrelled because centuries ago, two families of cranes came together. May I ask your name?"

"I am Lady MacCavity," I replied. And so as not to be outdone in the matter of pedigree, I swished my tail and added, "Of that Ilk."

"But of course. Delighted to meet you," said the crane. "And who is this young gentleman?"

"I am Colcu. Do you not remember me? I was with Abbot Colum Cille in the monastery in Ireland."

Friendship

"So you were. Do forgive me. One tends to meet so many when one holds a special position of responsibility in a monastery."

"What position was that?" I asked.

"He was Abbot Colum Cille's constant companion," Colcu interrupted with a vexed miaow. "So much so that on more than one occasion the abbot forgot to give me my food and milk."

"I do apologise," said Cronan. "But, as I recall, that sort of thing happened only when the abbot was busy transcribing ancient texts. You see, I often used to be at his side as he wrote. I acted as his secretary bird, so to speak. That was why I held such an important place in the monastic pecking order. Indeed, I remember that on one such occasion we were alone together in church where he was engrossed in copying a most valuable book that belonged to a neighbouring monastery. A monk, who had been sent by the abbot of that monastery to find out what was going on, spied on us through a crack in the door — but I soon saw him off."

"What did you do?" I asked, intrigued by his story.

"I poked at him with my beak through the crack in the door."

The Cats' Family Tree

"Yes, I heard about that," said Colcu. "A most unpleasant story. The monk told everyone in his monastery about it. He was not at all pleased."

"Indeed, he was not and neither was his abbot. In fact, the abbot sued for breach of copyright and the judgement went against Abbot Colum Cille who later decided to leave Ireland and come here."

"Why did you not come with him when he left Ireland, as I did?" asked Colcu.

"I had every intention of so doing but I got lost."

"Got lost? How?"

"Well, it's like this. When we are together as a flock, we cranes are expert dancers. If one of us begins a dance then we are all compelled to join in. Our dance consists of leaping up and down, running around, even pirouetting. We toss twigs and sticks in the air, catch them in our beaks and then bring our dance to a grand finale by shaking our wings vigorously. It really is a most remarkable display and is the envy of all other birds — and humans too."

"But what has this got to do with your getting lost?" I asked.

Friendship

"When I dance I put my whole self into it and have no thought of anything else. The fact is that during one such dance I was so filled with enthusiasm that I pirouetted myself out of the flock, and continued pirouetting, leaping and bounding, until I found that I was all alone with no idea of where I was. By the time I got back to the monastery Abbot Colum Cille and his monks had gone and were well on their way here. Of course, I flew in pursuit but then I encountered a dreadful storm and crashed down on a rock, breaking a wing in the process. It's taken me ages to get here and I'm quite exhausted. Could you tell me – have I landed on the right island? Is Abbot Colum Cille here?"

"Yes, you have and the abbot is here," said Colcu. "We all arrived here some time ago."

"All except me," I said. "This is the island of Iou. It's where I was born." I turned to Colcu. "Did I ever tell you that this is MacCavity land?"

"You did. Quite often." And he gave a long yawn.

"So I've finally got here!" cried Cronan. "I've persevered and at long last I've found my good friend, Abbot Colum Cille!"

The Cats' Family Tree

At that moment one of the monks reappeared and spoke to the crane. "Cronan Grus-Grus, Abbot Colum Cille says that I am to treat you as I would treat a pilgrim guest, and that I am to take you in my arms and nurse you back to health."

"There, I knew that all would be well again," exclaimed a very contented Cronan and he made a sound rather like a trumpet.

After three days his wing was fully recovered and off he flew, but not before putting in a few hours' work as secretary bird to Abbot Colum Cille. He arrived back from his trip about a week later, weary and dishevelled, but at least he had both wings intact.

"I've had a most frightening experience!" he cried. "I was happily flying around the island of Eth when what did I see but an enormous whale, a monster whale, a most frightening whale, the like of which I have never seen before!"

"What is a whale?" I asked.

"It's a big fish," Cronan replied.

"No, it is not a fish," said Colcu, impatiently. "It is a mammal."

Friendship

"A mammal?" exclaimed Cronan.

"Yes. MacCavity and I are mammals. That's because we grew inside our mothers' bodies and were fed by their blood, and then when we were born they fed us with their milk. I heard one of the monks say that this is a sign of how God feeds his people. You see, God led the people of Israel into the Promised Land where milk and honey flow. Jesus, God's only Son, feeds his people with his body and blood and leads them to the eternal life that he promises to all who believe in him."

"My mother hatched me from an egg," observed Cronan, "and then kept me safe under her wings."

"Neither is that image without its spiritual significance," Colcu replied, brightly. "Jesus longed to gather the children of Jerusalem as a hen gathers her chicks under her wings. Of course," he continued, turning his attention to me, "if you were a Church Cat as I am, you would also have access to these spiritual vignettes."

"I thought I was a Church Cat," I replied. "I've been living here with you in the monastery all these months, haven't I?"

"That's true, but you are still a cat–echumen, so to speak.

The Cats' Family Tree

However, I am confident that in due course you will qualify to receive the full status of Church Cat."

"I shall not disappoint your expectations," I replied proudly.

"Never mind all that," interjected Cronan crossly. "What about this whale?"

"Ah, yes, the whale," said Colcu. "Well, in my opinion it could be either a *Balaenoptera acutorostrata* or even a *Hyperoodon ampullatus*."

"Would you mind translating?" I asked.

"Of course not. Forgive me if I appear pretentious, but having been a Church Cat in a monastic community for some time, I am now, even though I say so myself, something of a Latinist. The first is commonly called a minke or piked whale and the second a northern bottle-nosed. Now, since Cronan described it as 'enormous, monstrous and frightening' I'm inclined to opt for the northern bottle-nosed."

By now Cronan was getting very agitated. "Does it really matter what kind of whale it is? The point is that Brother Berach intends to sail to the island of Eth tomorrow. I really think someone should warn him about the whale."

Friendship

"Which one is Brother Berach?" I asked.

"There are two Brothers who look alike," Cronan replied. "He is one of them."

"Thank you for identifying him so precisely," I said.

"Don't mention it," said Cronan. "I know what I shall do. I shall tell Abbot Colum Cille so that in the morning when Brother Berach asks for his blessing on the voyage he can advise him not to cross over by the open sea but to skirt around the smaller islands so as to avoid the whale."

And so that is what happened. But, sad to relate, Brother Berach did not heed Abbot Colum Cille's advice. He made straight for the island of Eth and, sure enough, the mighty whale rose up from the sea and caused such havoc to the waves that the boat nearly capsized. Colcu, Cronan and I watched as Berach and his companions arrived back at the monastery, soaked to the skin and pale with fright.

"That's what comes of being a 'know-all'," observed Cronan. "I've heard that another monk, Brother Baithene, has now decided to sail to Eth. He needs to have wisdom as his companion if he is not to make the same mistake."

"... a most frightening whale."

Friendship

"We could be his companions," suggested Colcu. "Cats are well known for their wisdom."

"Indeed we are," I said.

"What an excellent idea," said Cronan.

And so we agreed that Cronan would fly ahead of the boat and that Colcu and I would each act as a lookout since, of course, cats not only have acute hearing and sense of smell, they also see things that no human sees.

The next morning the boat, manned by a few monks, set sail for the island of Eth under the helm of Brother Baithene. Having been forewarned of the whale by Abbot Colum Cille he steered the boat across the open sea towards the smaller islands. Colcu and I stood on our hind legs against one side of the boat, peering out to sea. Then, all at once, we stiffened and growled in unison. On the horizon was the whale! We miaowed vigorously and trotted up and down the deck, trying to draw the monks' attention. But no one seemed to notice or to have any interest in what we were trying to tell them until, after what seemed like an age, one of the monks cried out, "Look! There's the whale and it's coming closer! What will we do? God save us!"

The Cats' Family Tree

Suddenly there was a flapping of wings and Cronan landed on the deck beside us. "No need to panic," he said. "You had all forgotten about me, but I've been very busy. I don't just fly around doing nothing, you know. I've been talking to the whale. His name is Walafrid and he's a very nice whale."

"That's not how you described him before," I exclaimed.

"It just shows that we must never judge on appearance only," replied Cronan. "Walafrid told me that all he wants is to make friends. He's rather lonely, you see, as he has lost his family. I know all about being lost, as I've told you before, and so I have promised to be his friend. Look! There he is. Watch him plunge beneath the waves. He's happy and contented now that he has a friend."

From that time on no one was ever afraid of Walafrid again. Cronan visited him frequently and fed him with various snippets of news from the mainland. But one day he told Cronan that, as much as he enjoyed his friendship, he wanted to be with his family again and wondered if Cronan could help him find them. After spending a long time flying around and searching, Cronan eventually found Walafrid's family a long way out into the ocean. He then guided him to that place and Walafrid was happily reunited with his friends and relations.

Friendship

As for Colcu and me, well, after spending some time on Eth exploring new territory we returned with Brother Baithene to our monastery on Iou. In due course I became an established Church Cat. And that is how I have come to write, or rather dictate, this little story. A monk who wishes to remain anonymous kindly agreed to receive dictation from me. He is an excellent scribe, as most monks are. Indeed, he spends much of his time in the monastic scriptorium, the special writing room for copying and illustrating biblical texts. He is rather anxious, however, that I should now bring my story to an end as the time is drawing near to the *Magnum Silentium* – the Great Silence – during which no monk worth his salt would be seen outside his cell.

And so I shall finish my little story by telling you what happened to Cronan. He stayed with Abbot Colum Cille for many years as his secretary bird until finally, having received a pension, together with a whole range of benefits and services, he returned to rejoin his flock in Ireland with whom he spent many a happy day teaching the younger birds to pirouette.

The Cats' Family Tree

"Was Lady MacCavity really my ancestor and was Colcu really the ancestor of Ko-Ko?" I asked Goldilocks as she turned the last page of this heavenly manuscript.

"Most definitely," she replied, "and very privileged ancestors too. They were evidently good friends of Saint Columba."

"Who is Saint Columba?" asked Ko-Ko.

"Why, Abbot Colum Cille of course. Columba is the Latin name given to him by Saint Adamnan who, towards the end of the seventh century, wrote about his life. Saint Adamnan was the ninth abbot of the monastery on the island of Iou or Hii – Iona as it was later called. Saint Columba's name means 'Dove'. Doves are simple and innocent birds."

"I doubt if the collared doves that fly around the church garden fit neatly into that description," I said. "On the contrary, they take over the bird tables and the smaller birds have to fight to get at the food."

"Since when, may I ask, have cats been concerned about the fair distribution of bird food?" enquired Goldilocks.

"It is merely an observation," I purred. "I miss nothing that happens in the garden."

Friendship

"How smart of you," Goldilocks said. "You will have noticed, of course, that when MacCavity and Colcu offered to accompany Brother Baithene to the island of Eth – or the island of Tiree as it is known today – they were proud of their wisdom as cats?"

"Of course," I said. "And not without reason."

"Quite so. But are you aware that wisdom is a gift of the Holy Spirit?"

"Oh yes, very much so. In fact, from my conversations with Saint Hubert I know that there are seven gifts of the Holy Spirit: wisdom, understanding, counsel, fortitude, knowledge, piety and fear of the Lord."

"Excellent," she replied. "Well, it so happens that your ancestors were also aware of these gifts and brought them into their memoirs. Indeed, the story that I have just related contains within it lessons on the gifts of wisdom, understanding and counsel. For example, Brother Baithene sought counsel from Saint Columba. He then acted wisely on the advice he received and showed respect to Walafrid the whale. You see, if people understand that they are to love and respect all of God's creation it helps them to live good and holy lives and to act with true wisdom."

The Cats' Family Tree

"Something like the understanding between me and Philonous the pheasant?" asked Ko-Ko.

"What understanding is that?"

"Well, if Philonous and I confront each other we both understand that one of us has to make the first move."

"That's not quite what I meant," said Goldilocks. "Can you tell me who did not act wisely in the story I have read to you?"

Friendship

"Well, it's pretty obvious, isn't it?" Ko-Ko replied. "It was Brother Berach, of course."

"You are absolutely right. It is always wise to be willing to learn from others, but it is never wise to be a 'know-all', especially with a saint – or indeed with a whale."

"Thank you for explaining these things to us," I said. "And now, could you tell us – is the monastery still on Iona?"

"The monastery which Saint Columba and his monks built, with the help of MacCavity and Colcu of course, is no longer there, but in its place is Iona Abbey and that is very old. It was built in the early thirteenth century. Every year very many people go to Iona, some as visitors, some as pilgrims. Near the main door of the abbey is a little chapel and this is Saint Columba's shrine. It is believed to be the site of his grave."

"Does anyone know the place where our ancestors first met?" Ko-Ko asked.

"Oh yes," said Goldilocks. "Saint Columba and his monks are believed to have landed on the south of the island at the 'Bay of the Coracle' or 'Saint Columba's Bay'. It is a very beautiful, wild place and that would

The Cats' Family Tree

have been where Lady MacCavity and Colcu met."

"Does my ancestor's story give any special message?" I asked.

"I think it tells us about the meaning of true friendship," Goldilocks replied. "At first MacCavity did not want Colcu in her territory and made him most unwelcome. But after their initial hostilities Colcu offered a paw of friendship. As a result, he and MacCavity were reconciled and became the best of friends. Later they made friends with Cronan the crane in his distress, and Cronan, in turn, became a friend to Walafrid the whale and helped him to find his family and other friends. To be a true friend to another is to share in God's love in a very special way."

I sat up, stretched out my front paws, and, grateful that now I knew something of my roots, decided to roll in the grass. Then I sat up again, yawned and had a wash. "When are we to expect another story?" I asked.

"I am rather busy at the moment," said Goldilocks. "It's well past the beginning of the new liturgical year and I'm late in sending in my heavenly returns. These refer to visits made to the cemetery, prayers offered by visitors, conversion experiences and so forth. But I assure

Friendship

you that I shall attend to the matter as soon as I can. However, it will be worth the wait. The next story is told by Ko-Ko's ancestor, Cogitosus. He was a friend of Saint Cuthbert to whom he dictated his story at Lindisfarne many centuries ago."

"Have you ever seen anything like that before?"

Chapter Two

Courage
by Cogitosus of Lindisfarne

My name is Cogitosus. I am the resident cat in the monastery at Lindisfarne in Northumbria, and live here with my feline friend of many years' standing, Macrina. My story is about the time when we lived on Farne Island, some miles out at sea, with a priest called Cuthbertus. He was the Prior of Lindisfarne, but he sailed over to the island in the year 676. About four years later the monks took us from the mainland to be his companions, as they

The Cats' Family Tree

knew how much he loved all animals. The monks had helped him to build a small dwelling and chapel. When we arrived they made an opening in the door for us. It is called a *janua felis*, or "door of the cat". It flapped up and down as we went in or out and so I suppose one could describe it as a "cat flap".

In the monastery on the mainland the monks awaken before the crack of dawn to the sound of a bell. Bells play a large part in your daily life if you are a monk. A bell not only wakes you up, it also summons you to prayer, or tells you that it is time to eat or to work or to have some recreation or to go to bed. Over on the island, of course, there are no bells. Instead, Macrina and I fulfilled that function by waking Cuthbertus up at variable times during the night. We did this by climbing on top of him as he lay asleep, gently tapping his face with our paws, walking over his head and body, miaowing, or simply sitting on his chest, purring and staring at him until he opened his eyes. We came to the conclusion that our usefulness in this regard probably prompted the monks to take us to the island. How else would Cuthbertus have known when to get up? Mind you, he did not always need our help for, as you shall presently see, he had a tendency not to go to bed at all but to spend the whole night in prayer.

Courage

The function of bells is also displaced on the island by the presence of great flocks of birds whose combined noise possibly equals that of all the bells in the world. There are eider ducks and Arctic terns. They nest in the grass and Macrina and I spent many an hour watching them, just as we watched the puffins nesting in their burrows. Then there are shags and cormorants nesting high on the ledges of the Whin Sill, while razorbills, fulmars, guillemots and kittiwakes nest in places that are inaccessible even to Macrina and me.

Near the little dwelling was a stone cross into which beautiful images had been carved. One day Macrina and I were sleeping underneath this cross after we had accompanied Cuthbertus on his daily walk around the island. We had covered a fair distance and as Macrina and I had been busily occupied in chasing each other, we were exhausted, but suddenly we were awakened by the sound of a shrill voice.

"Look at those birds flying around – how I wish that I could fly!"

We looked, and looked again, but could see nothing, other than two kittiwakes flying above us. We both agreed that the best thing to do was to go back to sleep.

The Cats' Family Tree

However, within minutes we were woken up again.

"I should have wings, you know. Angels are known and admired for their wings."

The voice came from a small angel carved in the stone cross.

"My name is Aurea Coma or Golden Hair," the angel continued. "I belong to a rather exclusive branch of the angelic family tree. We are known as 'apterous angels' as we don't have any wings. Of course, this does not prevent us from doing all the things winged angels do. It just takes us a little longer to do them, that's all."

"How interesting," I replied. "How long have you been here?"

"Oh, for about thirty years or so, I would think. I was brought over to the island when Saint Aidan was Bishop of Lindisfarne. He had founded the monastery in 635 on the invitation of the King of Northumbria, Saint Oswald, but he used to come here to find solitude and peace. Something to do with bells, I believe. I am rather surprised that you have not noticed me before now. I thought cats noticed everything."

Courage

"We do, of course," said Macrina. "But we are more inclined to notice things that move." She had just finished speaking when all at once a mighty bird appeared in the sky and circled above us. "Oh, my goodness," she cried. "Here's something that moves and moves swiftly. It's much bigger than us. We had better run for it!" But the bird had already landed on a nearby rock and was sitting there glaring at us. It was a very big bird indeed. We arched our backs simultaneously and prepared for the worst.

"Hello," said the bird. "There's no need to be afraid."

"May we ask who you are?" we enquired, nervously.

"You may, most certainly. I am Elfleda and I am an eagle."

"An eagle!" we cried, and we arched our backs again.

"There, there," said Elfleda soothingly. "No need for that. I've no intention of doing you any harm."

"That is most comforting," I said. How very strange, I thought, for an eagle to leave its territory in the mountains and fly so far south. "May we also ask what brings you to these parts?"

"Well, it so happens that Cuthbertus and I are old friends. I fly down to see him whenever the opportunity arises.

The Cats' Family Tree

You see, our friendship goes back a long way to the time when he was Prior of Melrose, much further north of here."

"We are also friends of Cuthbertus," I said.

"Any friend of his is a friend of mine," Elfleda replied.

"Thank goodness for that," said Macrina with undisguised relief. "How did you and Cuthbertus become friends?"

"It all happened like this," said Elfleda. "Cuthbertus frequently travelled into the hill country to visit the people, to preach, and to celebrate Mass and the other sacraments. One day, he and another monk had travelled many miles and they were tired and hungry. His companion felt too weak to continue but Cuthbertus encouraged him to carry on because he was sure that God would provide them with food. Now, who do you think appeared on the scene at that moment?"

"Could it have been you?" I asked – mainly to humour her, as I still wasn't too sure of her intentions towards us.

"Indeed it was," said Elfleda, proudly. "It just so happened that I had caught an extremely large and fat fish but

Courage

as I flew down to the ground my mind was on other things and I forgot about the fish with the result that I inadvertently released it from my grip and it fell to earth."

"How unfortunate," I said. "But never mind. All of us have these momentary lapses. Even I have been known to release a mouse unintentionally."

"Have you indeed?" said Elfleda, somewhat irritated by the interruption. "If I may continue? Well, what happened then was that the other monk seized the fish as it lay on the ground and took it to Cuthbertus. What do you think Cuthbertus did?"

"I haven't the slightest idea," I replied. I yawned and began washing myself – as we cats frequently do.

"Cuthbertus told him off, that's what he did. He told him that he should have given me a portion of the fish since I had provided it. After he and his companion had eaten their share of the fish, he insisted that they should take the rest to a poor family to whom they were making their journey, but not before I had been provided with my portion. That is why he and I have been friends ever since."

The Cats' Family Tree

"May I make a contribution to the conversation?" The question came from Aurea Coma, who had been listening in the background. None of us answered, but she continued nonetheless. "I too hold Cuthbertus as a special friend. In point of fact, he is on intimate terms with all the angelic family, winged or not winged."

"How is that?" I asked.

"Well, you see, from the time he was a youth Cuthbertus has received visions from one or other of my family individually, but more often than not from a number of us combined in a heavenly chorus. That's the sort of thing we do, you know, as we find it provides an excellent musical background to whatever message we are commissioned to convey. I believe the first time this happened was when he was guarding the sheep on the hills near Melrose and witnessed one of our angelic choirs accompanying the soul of Saint Aidan to paradise. When he came to this island it was believed that evil spirits dwelt here. But Cuthbertus armed himself with the helmet of salvation, the shield of faith and the sword of the spirit – that is to say, the word of God – and with the help of the angelic army he banished the evil spirits."

"From where did he obtain this military equipment?" I asked.

Courage

"I speak metaphorically," said Aurea Coma with a look of disdain.

"I have heard that an angel helped him to build his hermitage here on the island," said Macrina.

"That is true," Aurea Coma replied, "but I wasn't going to mention it."

"Why ever not?"

"Because it was... " She hesitated.

"Because it was you?" asked Macrina.

"You?" asked Elfeda.

"Yes," she replied, coyly. "Me. I helped Cuthbertus."

"But you are an image carved in stone," I said. "Images carved in stone don't do that kind of thing... do they?"

"Most images don't, but I am not like most images. I am an angel and angels are not confined to time and space."

"Even though you can't fly?"

"You don't need to fly if you are helping to build a hermitage. Everyone knows that," said Aurea Coma with a look now bordering on despair.

The Cats' Family Tree

"I suppose so," I said.

And with that, the conversation came to an abrupt end as none of us could think of anything else to say. When there seems nothing else to say it is always a good thing to say nothing. Elfleda flapped her powerful wings, took off and soared high into the sky. Aurea Coma went back to sleep. Macrina yawned and stretched out her front paws. I had a wash. It was time for our dinner. We both ran back to the hermitage as fast as we could.

Early next morning, having awakened Cuthbertus in our usual fashion and after he had given us our breakfast, we went out through our *janua felis* and mooched around. All at once we stopped short in our tracks. Two young ravens were busily engaged in removing straw from the roof of the hermitage.

"Just a minute!" we cried. "You can't do that!"

"Why not?" said one of the birds. "We've come up here from Brigantia. I'm Ravennus and this 'ere is Rasyphus. We want this straw for our holiday home."

"That's no excuse for taking the roof from over our heads. That straw is there to keep Cuthbertus dry – not to mention us – when the weather is bad."

Courage

"Weather's fine at present and in any case I reckon as you soon won't be in need of it, 'appen," said Ravennus.

"Whatever do you mean?"

"Well, rumour is that Cuthbertus has been elected bishop. So he won't be living here, will he? Neither will you, 'appen."

"Elected bishop?" I cried. "Not living here? It's the first we have heard of it."

"That's the way it is these days in t'Church. Those most affected by decisions are usually last to know."

"Aye, you're right," Rasyphus nodded in agreement.

"But even Cuthbertus hasn't said anything to us about it," we replied.

"Well, he wouldn't. He'd be told to keep it to 'isself, 'appen. Anyway, he doesn't want to be a bishop, so I've 'eard."

"I've 'eard that an' all," Rasyphus again nodded in agreement.

"Doesn't want to be a bishop?" I exclaimed. "Why ever not?"

The Cats' Family Tree

"Who'd want to be a bishop these days? I mean, there's been all these 'ere problems over date of Easter and suchlike, and then there's all these 'ere wars that keep breaking out."

"Aye, that keep breaking out," repeated Rasyphus.

"I can't say I blame him for not wanting to be a bishop," Ravennus continued. "Mind you, 'appen decision will be taken out of his hands. I've 'eard as how King Ecgfrith is coming over here a' Tuesday this week to try and persuade him and I can't see Cuthbertus going against what t'king wants him to do, can you?"

We had to agree that we couldn't.

The ravens then picked up where they had left off and continued to take straw from the roof but as they did so Cuthbertus himself came out of his hermitage.

"I wonder what he is going to do," said Macrina. "Oh, look. He's saying something to them. Well, I never. They are ignoring him. Isn't that so typical of youngsters these days? Just a minute, he's banishing them from the island and – goodness me – they are flying away."

But later that same day they were back again. Macrina

Courage

and I watched as this time they helped themselves to the barley that Cuthbertus had sown.

"Th'early bird catches the worm, eh?" said Ravennus.

"But you are not catching worms. You are stealing the barley," Macrina exclaimed.

"Worms or barley – it's still a good catch."

"Aye, a good catch," echoed Rasyphus.

"It's just what we need for our holiday," Ravennus explained.

"Never mind your holiday," I remonstrated. "You are being very selfish and inconsiderate."

"You and t'other cat are fine ones to talk," Ravennus retorted. "Why, I were watching you only t'other day when you caught a duckling. You took it into t'house through this 'ere small door of yours. I saw Cuthbertus come out, clasping duckling in one hand and caressing it wi' t'other. He were telling it as how he were going to take it back to its mother, like. Well, he goes into water and he slips, doesn't he? Soaked to skin, he were, and he had a few fish stuck in his habit an' all. But he got duckling back to its mother and family, he did. Now, you

"Each carried a small piece of hog's lard."

Courage

weren't being very considerate then, were you? I reckon as how you caused Cuthbertus and the duckling a lot of unnecessary trouble, 'appen."

"Aye, trouble," said Rasyphus.

"I didn't think of it in that way," I admitted. "We had intended it as a gift."

"Perhaps we all need to ask Cuthbertus for his forgiveness," Macrina suggested.

"Perhaps we do," said Ravennus.

" 'Appen," Rasyphus added.

And that is what happened. Three days later Ravennus and Rasyphus returned. Each carried a small piece of hog's lard and they placed these at the feet of Cuthbertus as tokens of their sorrow. He readily forgave them and invited them to stay on the island for as long as they wished – which, of course, they did. Macrina and I decided that the best way we could show our sorrow for having caused him so much trouble was to comfort him as only cats can. Macrina curled up on his knee and I at his feet. There we stayed for a long time while Cuthbertus sat and prayed.

The Cats' Family Tree

But throughout that day he seemed troubled. In the evening we saw him walking towards the shore, but we hardly took any notice, as we were preoccupied with observing the goings-on of various birds on the cliffs. Many hours later we went into the hermitage expecting to find him asleep – but he was not there. We wondered where he could be. We trotted off to a small sandy inlet in search of him. When we arrived we stopped short in amazement.

Cuthbertus was almost fully immersed in the sea. The sound of the waves accompanied him as, with outstretched arms, he sang the praises of God. At other times he prayed silently. Macrina and I watched in wonder. All night long Cuthbertus stayed in the sea and then, when dawn appeared on the sea's horizon, he came out of the waters and knelt on the pebbles, his prayer uninterrupted.

"Why is he doing this?" Macrina whispered.

"I don't know," I whispered back.

"Well, I do," said a voice. It belonged to an eider duck that was hidden in a large tuft of grass. "I've seen him pray in this way many times before, especially when he has to make an important decision. I've heard that they

Courage

want to make him a bishop and so I expect he's asking God's help on his decision."

"It seems – how shall I put it? It seems... a somewhat dramatic way of doing things," I observed.

"Dramatic it may be," responded the duck, whose name, we discovered later, was Dulcitius Dux, "but it's far better than sneaking up and grabbing a duckling as you did recently. That was my duckling you stole, incidentally. I'm the father."

"I'm so very sorry," I said. "But Cuthbertus did return the duckling to your wife, didn't he?"

"No thanks to you. Anyway, that's the sort of thing Cuthbertus does. He loves all of us who live on the island, and we love him." Then, with a sudden quack, he added, "See what I mean?" and, as if emulating the Roman general whose name he bore, he led a previously hidden company of ducks – and us – towards the edge of the cliff. "Look down there on the shore!" he commanded. "Look at what's happening."

We peered over the edge of the cliff and there, coming out of the sea and moving towards Cuthbertus, were two creatures that resembled very large weasels.

The Cats' Family Tree

"Are they sea monsters?" asked Macrina.

"They are otters," Dulcitius replied and then added sternly, "keep quiet and see what happens now."

The otters stretched themselves out in front of Cuthbertus, warming his feet with their breath and trying to dry him with their fur, and then, having received his blessing, they returned to the waves from which they came.

"There!" exclaimed Dulcitius. "What do you think of that? Have you ever seen anything like that before?"

"No," we replied. "But what does it mean?" I asked.

"It means that the otters are not afraid of Cuthbertus and that they came to give him help and comfort."

Being a cat and, like all cats, having profound thoughts, I persisted with my question. "Does it have a deeper meaning?"

"Probably it does," said Dulcitius Dux. "But I am not a philosopher, nor am I a theologian: I'm a duck. Why don't you ask the angel about it?"

Later that day we went to see Aurea Coma. Macrina and I sat before the stone cross and miaowed so as to wake her up.

Courage

"There's no need for that," she said. "I may look to be asleep, but I'm not. It's the way I've been fashioned by the monk who carved me into the stone. Now before you go any further I know exactly what you are going to ask me. I've been watching everything from my vantage point here. Indeed, little escapes my attention."

"Then you will have seen Cuthbertus praying in the sea and the otters as they tried to help him?" we asked.

"Oh yes, all of that," she replied. "And you want to know what it all means, do you not? Well, it's quite simple. As Dulcitius so rightly observed, Cuthbertus was asking God to help him make the right decision. As you already know from those tiresome ravens, Cuthbertus doesn't want to be a bishop. That's why he seemed so troubled of late. But he has remembered that the Lord, on the eve of his crucifixion, prayed that he would do his Father's will, and so Cuthbertus prayed with the Lord's example before him."

"And does he now know what God wants him to do?" Macrina asked.

"Yes, he does, and he is at peace."

"And what about the otters?" I asked. "What did they have to do with it?"

67

The Cats' Family Tree

"They fought back their fear and gave him warmth and comfort. He, in turn, saw that what they did was a sign of heaven where fear is no more and so, through them, he overcame his fear of becoming a bishop. You see, the demons Cuthbertus banished from the island came back and they are still here. Indeed, they are everywhere in the world, not least within the hearts of men and women. But, when we call on God's love in prayer, and through the death and resurrection of Jesus, the power of the devil and all his demons will not overwhelm us."

"So Cuthbertus will leave the island," I said. "What will happen to us?"

"I'm sure that he will take you with him. Bishops have to get up early too, you know, and your assistance will be invaluable to him."

And so it was that Cuthbertus became a bishop and took us back to Lindisfarne. He is now heavily occupied in doing all the things that bishops do, but Macrina and I know that he wants to return to the island one day, as do we. Who knows what God has planned for us? In the meantime, a young monk named Edfrith is busily engaged in drawing preparatory sketches for a book of the Gospels he intends to write and illustrate. He has kindly written these memoirs at our behest and has even drawn sketches of Macrina and me for use in his illustrations. Now we must bring our memoirs to a close, as it would never do to let Bishop Cuthbertus oversleep, would it?

Goldilocks put down the manuscript and sighed. "All this talk of sleep has made me feel quite drowsy. However, I must say that I was delighted these memoirs contain reference to my own angelic family and, in particular, to Aurea Coma. Her relationship with your ancestors was rather like the relationship that we ourselves enjoy, was it not?"

"I was struck by the similarity," said Ko-Ko.

"Quite so. But there is one thing I must stress and it is this. Aurea Coma was fashioned to look as if she were asleep. There the similarity ends. I never appear to be asleep. I always look wide awake and alert."

"Indeed, you do," I agreed. "Even though I expect that you are now going to have a siesta, I won't know that you are having one and neither will anyone else."

The Cats' Family Tree

"They certainly will not," she yawned and thereupon fell asleep.

"What are we going to do now?" I asked Ko-Ko. "Did Macrina and Cogitosus return to the island? How are we going to find out?"

"I know," said Ko-Ko. "Let's go and ask Saint Hubert. He will know all about it."

That night we trotted into the church and sat underneath Saint Hubert's stained glass window.

"Hello, Saint Hubert. Could you possibly help us?" I asked. Then I proceeded to tell him about the memoirs of Cogitosus.

"It is quite remarkable that your ancestors knew Saint Cuthbert so well," he observed. "Of course, Cuthbert and I are very good friends. I became Bishop of Maestricht in 705 and that was only twenty years after he became Bishop of Lindisfarne, you know. Yes indeed, we often reminisce about times past."

"Did he ever go back to Farne Island?" Ko-Ko asked. "And did Cogitosus and Macrina go with him?"

Courage

"Oh yes, he did and I believe that they accompanied him. He died on Farne Island and entered heaven on 20th March 687. He had wanted a simple burial, but the monks took his body back to Lindisfarne and his shrine became a great centre of pilgrimage for many years. But when the Vikings invaded, the monks moved away for safety and took Saint Cuthbert's body with them. For a long time his body had no permanent place of burial, but in 1104 he was laid to rest in Durham Cathedral. Incidentally," he said to Ko-Ko, "you may be interested to know that your ancestor's memoir is not the only literary work about Saint Cuthbert. Saint Bede, who was born in 673 – fourteen years before Cuthbert died – also wrote about him. For most of his life Saint Bede was a monk of the monastery of Saint Paul in Jarrow. He completed writing his *Life of Saint Cuthbert* in 721 and his most famous work, his *History of the English Church and People*, in 731. Of course it goes without saying that Saint Bede is also a very dear friend of mine."

"One would expect no less," I replied. "But did he make mention of Macrina and Cogitosus?"

"Not that I recall."

"Do you know what happened to them?"

The Cats' Family Tree

"The evidence is rather unclear on this point," Saint Hubert answered, "but I have every confidence that the monks took great care of them."

"Goldilocks said that the story about MacCavity and Colcu who lived with Saint Columba on Iona had some thoughts on the gifts of the Holy Spirit," Ko-Ko said. "Does this story have any such thoughts?"

"Indeed it does," Saint Hubert replied. "Cuthbert obviously lived under the guidance of the Holy Spirit; he had great courage in the face of difficulties, he studied the scriptures, and his life was centred on prayer and on caring for others, especially the poor. So in this story we have, in particular, the gifts of fortitude, knowledge, piety and fear of the Lord."

"By 'fear of the Lord' do you mean that he was afraid of God?" I asked.

"Not afraid as a mouse might well be afraid of you," he replied. "Not that kind of fear, but a fear that comes from being aware of our own sinfulness compared to God's holiness and goodness. It seems that all through his life Saint Cuthbert struggled with many temptations to turn away from God, but he loved God with all his heart and he knew that God loved him from all eternity.

Courage

He remembered that Jesus often told his disciples not to be afraid, and so Cuthbert put his trust in God's love and mercy, and in Jesus, the Saviour of the world."

"Does any of this apply to cats?" I asked.

"It does in so far as God created you and Ko-Ko and all your ancestors and loves you because God loves all that he has made."

"And do we have any of the gifts of the Spirit?"

"Cats are brimming over with so many gifts that it would be impossible to count them all," he said.

"How verrrry kind," I purred.

Later that evening Ko-Ko and I went back to see Goldilocks. "She's sure to be awake by now," I said. But when we arrived at the foot of her plinth and greeted her there was no response.

"I think I should wake her up," I said. And so I miaowed loudly and frequently. But she did not stir. Ko-Ko now jumped onto the plinth and attacked her feet. That did the trick.

"Why is it," Goldilocks asked, "that cats always assume that it is their privilege to wake one up? I would never

The Cats' Family Tree

even think of waking either of you when you were asleep and I very much doubt if the priest would do so either."

"The priest sometimes wakes me up," I said.

"And me," said Ko-Ko.

"May I ask under what circumstances?" said Goldilocks.

"If we happen to have come in at night and are asleep either before the fire or in our chairs, he strokes us before he retires for the night and he asks God to bless us."

"Surely you don't object to that?"

"Usually not," I replied, "though it still disturbs our sleep."

"But we get our own back," said Ko-Ko. "We frequently jump onto his bed in the early morning and lick his face or tap his nose with our paws."

"In that case, I'm rather relieved that I remain here day and night," said Goldilocks. "However, please tell me. What pressing matter urges you to wake me up now?"

"We just wanted to say that we know what happened to our ancestors after Saint Cuthbert became a bishop. Saint Hubert told us. He also gave us some spiritual insights into my ancestor's story," said Ko-Ko.

Courage

"Excellent!" she replied. "I'm always pleased when didactic duties are devolved."

"Have the Recording Angels discovered any more of our ancestors' memoirs?" I enquired.

"They have indeed," she replied. "The next memoirs will come from your ancestor, Miss Mac. She lived in a remote and enchanting valley in Wales and was a friend of Saint Melangell who was a princess and became an abbess. Her shrine was a place of pilgrimage and a sanctuary for many kinds of animals and wildlife for hundreds of years."

"When may we hear the story?" I asked.

"As soon as I've caught up on my interrupted sleep," said Goldilocks, "possibly in a week or two."

"I'm Dyfrig and I'm a dragon," the creature replied.

Chapter Three

Wisdom
by Mythanwy of Cwm Pennant

Cynllo and I crouched down and waited. On a rock by the side of the waterfall, at the head of the valley, a small creature with a long tail and scaly skin was basking in the sunshine. An hour or so passed by; but the creature did not move and neither did we. Another hour came and went. We decided to sit up and have a wash. As we did so, the creature moved, but ever so slightly.

The Cats' Family Tree

Cynllo was the first to break the silence. "Who are you and what are you?" he asked.

"I'm Dyfrig and I'm a dragon," the creature replied.

"A dragon!" Cynllo exclaimed. "A dragon! Don't be silly. You're not big enough to be a dragon."

"I'm a baby dragon. All dragons are babies when they are very, very young, you know."

"You're not a baby dragon, I tell you," Cynllo retorted. He paused, and after pausing he pondered. He looked over the creature, then he pondered again. Finally he said, "I know what you are. You're a lizard, not a dragon."

"No I'm not. My parents told me that I was a dragon, so I must be a dragon."

"Not at all," said Cynllo. "You are definitely a lizard. I imagine that when your parents called you a dragon they did so, not because you are a dragon, but probably because you were being naughty. When I was a kitten and I was fighting my brothers and sisters, my mother often called me a tiger. It didn't mean that I was a tiger; I have always been a tabby cat. She was simply scolding me for being naughty."

Wisdom

"I'm never naughty," said Dyfrig.

"Now look here," I interjected. "If Dyfrig thinks he is a dragon, where's the harm? If you go on like this you will hurt his feelings. Neither you nor I have ever seen a baby dragon, and, for all we know, he might well be what he says he is."

"But he is not a dragon!" Cynllo retorted. "My point is that you can't go through life telling others that you are what you are not."

"Humans do it all the time," I replied. "Has this fact escaped your attention? If it has, I'm rather surprised. Remember that we are cats and, as all cats do, we spend hours watching humans and scrutinising their foibles, do we not?"

"Well, I suppose you're right, Mythanwy," Cynllo replied. "Humans do tend to have exaggerated ideas about themselves. Perhaps it's best to let him believe he's a dragon and say no more about it."

"Thank you," said Dyfrig, and promptly went back to sleep.

Cynllo and I moved on from the waterfall and headed

The Cats' Family Tree

deeper into the valley. We trotted along the side of the stream and at regular intervals we stopped in our tracks to sniff the ground or to look around so as not to miss anything. It was near evening and everywhere was quiet and still. But then suddenly, in the distance, there was the sound of dogs barking. Then came the sound of horses galloping, then of men shouting, then of the huntsman's horn.

"My goodness, Mythanwy," whispered Cynllo. "Look over there on the hillside. It's a hare. The hunters are chasing a hare! Hide quickly!" We dived into the ferns and found a small opening from which we could see all that was going on.

The hare ran madly down the hillside before leaping into bushes and then disappearing into a wood. The hunters and their horses came to a halt, and then cantered off. All was quiet again.

We emerged from the ferns, yawned, stretched out our front paws, and then moved slowly and deliberately back towards the stream where we sat down. "I think it's time for us to get back to the lady who lives with us, Cynllo," I said. "She will have prepared our food by now."

Wisdom

We set off along the bank of the stream. It was a glorious evening in spring. Two lambs were ahead of us and in front of them a mother sheep and her lamb. As we trotted along so did they, gathering pace at each step. A pheasant decided to join us. This rather unusual procession of sheep, lambs, pheasant and cats then reached a curve in the stream, at which point a duck quacked loudly and made a hasty exit with her two ducklings from underneath the bank. The procession moved on. With a flurry of wings and many more quacks another duck and a dozen or so larger ducklings sped downstream. A cuckoo called. Two sheep on the other side of the river joined in the crescendo by bleating continuously as they moved towards a narrow part of the stream where they waded across to join their offspring. Then, all at once, the sheep and lambs ran off; the pheasant flew into a neighbouring field and was joined in flight and in a continuous cackling noise by numerous other pheasants that appeared as if out of nowhere. All that remained of the procession were Cynllo and I. How remarkable, I thought, that in the space of a few minutes the peace and tranquillity of the countryside had been shattered – and all because two cats had decided to go home for their meal.

The Cats' Family Tree

As we drew nearer to the clearing in the wood where we lived we heard a voice: "Mythanwy! Cynllo! Where are you? Come on! Your supper's ready!" It was the voice of the lady who lives with us. "Ah! There you are!" she said as we made our appearance. "Where have you been? I've not seen you all day. I was getting worried about you."

Now, before I go any further with my story, I think I should tell you who this lady is and where we live. The lady is a beautiful princess and her name is Melangell. We all live together in the Tanat Valley at Cwm Pennant deep in the heart of the Berwyn Mountains in the Principality of Powys. The events I am relating happened when Princess Melangell had lived here for fifteen years. Cynllo and I took over her accommodation when she rescued us because we had nowhere to live and we were only kittens. It was a small dwelling but we all got on extremely well and she was, and still is, most attentive to our needs.

Why, I hear you ask, did a princess live with two cats in a little dwelling deep in the mountains? Indeed, it was this very question that exercised our minds the following evening when Cynllo and I returned to the waterfall. We had hoped that Dyfrig would be there but he had disappeared.

Wisdom

"If he is a dragon," said Cynllo, "as he says he is, then he will grow to an enormous size and become very powerful."

"But yesterday you were certain that he was a lizard. What has made you change your mind?" I asked.

"I've not changed my mind. I'm certain he is a lizard. The problem is that I'm not absolutely certain."

"In that case, I would suggest that you have moral certainty," I replied, rather grandly.

"Moral certainty? What's that?"

"It means that you have no well-founded or reasonable doubt that he is a lizard. On the other hand, it's not totally impossible that he is a dragon."

"In other words, you are saying that I'm not absolutely certain," said Cynllo.

"Exactly."

"But that's what I said before."

"I was merely utilising a legal concept in order to put the matter into a logical framework," I purred.

The Cats' Family Tree

And with that, we both crouched down and gazed at the rock Dyfrig had occupied the previous day. We did this for some considerable time. Eventually I sat up and began washing my paws and then my ears. This, too, took some considerable time. Eventually I turned to Cynllo and miaowed. "Isn't it about time we moved on?" I said. "It's obvious that Dyfrig is not going to make an appearance."

"I suppose so," said Cynllo as he sat up. "But at least the time spent here has been an opportunity for reflection."

"Reflection on what?" I asked.

"On who we are and who we think we are," Cynllo replied. "I mean, Dyfrig thinks he is a dragon. But is he? We think that the lady who lives with us is a princess. But that's only because we have heard people in the village talking about her and saying that she's a princess. What if she isn't a real princess, but only thinks she is? Princesses don't usually live in small dwellings like ours, do they? And we are agreed, are we not, that humans tend to exaggerate their own importance?"

"Oh, come, come," I replied. "Are you not letting your thoughts run away with you? Of course she is a princess."

Wisdom

"Do you say this with absolute or moral certainty?" he asked, rather facetiously.

"With absolute certainty, of course. Why, only this morning I heard her praying for her family. You were asleep at the time. She mentioned her father by name. He is King Jowchel and his kingdom is in Ireland."

Cynllo made no reply. It was his turn to have a wash and he made the most of it, thereby giving himself plenty of time to think. He washed and he washed and when he had finished washing he said, "This still does not answer the question of why, if she is a princess, is she not living in a large dwelling rather than in a small one with no one else but us?" He swished his tail with a flourish. "How do you explain that?"

"Quite easily," I replied. "When she was speaking to the Lord in her prayers she said that she had given up everything for love of him and that she had left her home and family in Ireland and even the man she was going to marry. She said that she wanted to love the Lord above all else and to serve him and the Blessed Virgin in poverty and simplicity."

Cynllo crouched down again and gazed ahead. Obviously another of his ponderous moods, I thought — and indeed

The Cats' Family Tree

it was. He pondered for a very long time, at the end of which he said, "Well, Mythanwy, after thinking long and hard about it, and bearing in mind all that you have said, I am now convinced that the lady is a real princess. In fact, I can say that I have absolute..." I think he was going to say "absolute certainty about it", but suddenly his ears picked up and he whispered, "Listen. Isn't that the sound of a hunting horn?"

"You're right," I said. "And it's growing nearer and louder." In an instant, the dogs, the huntsmen and their horses appeared on the horizon of the hill. "Look!" I cried. "There's the hare. He's racing down the hill again. Oh, my goodness, he's coming towards us and the hunt is following him. We'd best make a run for it!"

The hare sped past us and ran along the bank of the stream towards the wood. We followed close behind, running as fast as our legs would carry us, and in hot pursuit came the hunt with dogs barking ferociously and horses galloping furiously. Sheep and lambs scattered in all directions. Pheasants and ducks flew off in noisy indignation.

First into the wood was the hare. "Quick, Mythanwy!" cried Cynllo. "Into the wood! The hunt won't follow us

Wisdom

there." But he was wrong. The hunters were determined not to let the hare escape again. On and on they rode, crashing through thickets and tearing off branches, the dogs barking and yelping all the time.

And then, all at once, we came upon a thicket of brambles. Nearby was Princess Melangell, kneeling in prayer. The hare scampered towards her and then disappeared into a fold in her long garment. "Follow him, Cynllo!" I cried. "The princess' robe will hide us as well!" We dived into the folds of her robe and remained there, perfectly still.

"Who are you?" whispered the hare from the adjoining fold of the robe.

"I think we should be the ones to ask that question of you," I whispered back. "After all, this is our princess and if any animals have a right to hide in the folds of her robe those animals are us."

"That's as may be," the hare replied. "But as we are all in mortal danger it doesn't really matter, does it?"

"I think one can have rather more than moral certainty on that point," observed Cynllo. "Indeed, I would go so far as to say one could have absolute certainty."

The Cats' Family Tree

"I suppose one could," I replied. "Anyway, it's nice to know who one's neighbours are. Just for the record, I'm Mythanwy and this is Cynllo."

"Pleased to meet you, I'm sure," said the hare. "I'm Hopcyn. But listen! The hunters are here. We had best keep quiet and still."

And then, all at once, very curious things began to happen. We peeped out from our hiding place and there was Hopcyn emerging fearlessly from underneath the princess' robe to face the snarling dogs. "Go on, hounds, don't waste time! Get the hare!" cried a man, obviously of noble rank, who was seated on a horse. But instead of attacking Hopcyn, the dogs howled and ran away. Then a huntsman attempted to blow his horn – but his hands stuck fast and there was not a sound. In a flash, Hopcyn lost no time and darted into the thicket.

"Well, I never!" exclaimed Cynllo. "These are strange events if ever there were."

The man of noble rank dismounted and approached Princess Melangell. He bowed slightly and introduced himself. "I am Brochwel Ysgithrog, Prince of Powys and Earl of Chester," he said. "How long have you lived here on my lands and why have you chosen this remote place?"

Wisdom

The princess gave a small curtsy. Of course, by so doing, she dislodged us from our snug accommodation in her robe and so we leapt into the thicket, crouched down and watched all that was going on. Hopcyn emerged from the back of the thicket and joined us.

Prince Brochwel listened intently as the princess told him who she was and why she had come to live at Cwm Pennant. When she had finished speaking, the prince thought deeply. At length he said, "I believe that I am standing in a holy place where heaven is joined to earth. Through your prayers, Princess Melangell, the Lord has chosen to give safe conduct and protection to this little wild hare, not to mention these two little cats." Cynllo and I purred in appreciation and Hopcyn thumped his foot. "Melangell, I believe that you are a true disciple of the Lord," the prince continued. "Therefore, I now give you these my lands for the service of God and as a place of refuge, not only for all people who are in any need, but also for hares and all wildlife – and, oh yes, also for cats."

"That's exceedingly good of him," said Hopcyn. "It means that I am not going to be hunted any more."

Cynllo and I looked at each other. "You realise, of course," I said, "that we won't be able to hunt him either."

"You realise, of course, that we won't be able to hunt him."

"You most certainly will not. And I can say that with absolute certainty!" exclaimed Hopcyn as he happily hopped away.

Prince Brochwel was true to his word. In the centre of a circle of ancient yew trees a little church has been built in Cwm Pennant, as have dwellings for the ladies who have joined Princess Melangell and who now live with her

Wisdom

as a community of Sisters, serving the Lord in poverty, prayer and simplicity. Their numbers have increased and the princess has become their abbess. Naturally, Cynllo and I are important members of this community and we have been given the status of Church Cats. We each fulfil our roles admirably by keeping the mice at bay and by spending many hours asleep in the church. Indeed, we are so highly respected for our work as Church Cats that when it came to writing these memoirs I was inundated with requests from the Sisters to take on the role of scribe. In the end I had no option but to assign to each Sister some form of participation in the work, either by penning a section or by feeding Cynllo and me whenever required, or by making a sisterly lap available for our necessary periods of sleep.

But what of Dyfrig who thought he was a dragon? Well, he has grown into a very large lizard indeed, and so he still thinks he is a dragon. To creatures smaller than he it probably seems that Dyfrig is a dragon. It all depends on your point of view, doesn't it?

And what of Hopcyn? It will probably come as no surprise when I tell you that just as Abbess Melangell's community has increased so has the colony of hares that came to join Hopcyn as soon as word spread of their

The Cats' Family Tree

immunity from being hunted. They now run around free of fear, as do all the animals, of which there are many – stoats and weasels, rabbits, field mice, badgers, foxes, and all kinds of birds including little owls, barn owls, herons, buzzards, to name but a few.

I should not end these memoirs without telling you that Hopcyn and the other hares have been given the name Wyn bach Melangell, which means "Melangell's lambs". It goes without saying that Cynllo says it isn't right for hares to be known as lambs when they are, in fact, hares. However, I have told him that I have not the slightest inclination to enter into another debate with him. I shall leave him to ponder the matter while I curl up and go to sleep on Abbess Melangell's lap.

"The question raised by Cynllo, about who we are and who we think we are, is quite interesting," Goldilocks commented as she finished reading the heavenly manuscript. "Don't you agree?"

Wisdom

"Yes, I do," I replied. "Is he saying that some people have illusions about themselves?"

"Well yes, he is rather," she said. "Of course, we angels don't suffer from any such illusions, and I expect the same is true for cats, is it not?"

"Indeed, it is. We are all very contented to be cats. That is why we purr such a lot, you know."

"Yes, I must say that I find your purrs quite soothing. You are most welcome to curl up on my lap and purr at any time."

"Thank you. I would if you were sitting down but," I pointed out, "you are always standing up."

"I can't help the way I've been made, can I?" she snapped.

"Of course not." I thought it best to be diplomatic. "I can always climb up onto your shoulder," I suggested. "It's always good to have a shoulder to purr on."

"Oh, would you? How very kind," she said, her angelic serenity regained.

"It will be a pleasure. I may find the folds of your long robe a trifle difficult to negotiate when climbing up but I'm sure I'll manage."

The Cats' Family Tree

"I'm sure you will. Indeed, my robe could serve the purpose of reminding you of Mythanwy's story as I expect the garment is similar in style to that worn by Melangell," she replied. "Have we not just learnt that her robe gave protection to Hopcyn the hare and to Cynllo and Mythanwy as the folds provided them with a place in which to hide?"

"Yes, we have," I agreed. "It's always helpful to find somewhere to hide. Ko-Ko and I have many hiding places in the garden. They give excellent cover and are most useful when the priest is out and about searching for us."

"But why do you hide from the priest? You, Ko-Ko and he are companions, are you not?"

"Yes, we are," replied Ko-Ko, "but we need to hold onto our independence. If he finds us, he invariably picks us up and interferes with whatever plans we have made."

"How extremely tiresome," Goldilocks observed. "Yet it could be said that even God seems to interfere with our plans at times. Think of Melangell. She was going to be married, but God had other plans for her and because she loved God so much she became a saint."

"Yes, I was going to ask you about that," I said. "Iona

Wisdom

and Lindisfarne became centres of pilgrimage. Did the same happen to Cwm Pennant where all these things took place?"

"It did. It has been a place of pilgrimage for more than a thousand years. It is named after the saint and is known as Pennant Melangell. Pennant means the 'head of the stream', the very same stream near where Mythanwy and Cynllo had their adventures."

"And is the church still there," asked Ko-Ko, "and the little dwelling where Saint Melangell lived with our ancestors?"

"Sadly their little dwelling has gone, as has the original wooden church in which your ancestors slept, but in their place is a church that was first built in the twelfth century. It is dedicated to Saint Melangell (who, incidentally, is also known as Saint Monacella) and many pilgrims go there to light candles and to pray before the saint's shrine."

"People light candles in front of Our Lady's statue here in Saint Hubert's," said Ko-Ko. "They put them in the thick layer of sand that covers the base of the candle stand. I find the sand particularly comfortable. Quite frequently I crouch down in it and observe what's going on, but only if no candles are burning – obviously."

The Cats' Family Tree

"Obviously," Goldilocks replied rather sniffily. "May I continue? As I was about to say, the shrine to Saint Melangell was destroyed at the time of the Reformation. In the last century it was rebuilt, using stones from the original shrine, and it is now as it was all those centuries ago. It is the only shrine of that period to have survived in Britain. In front of the shrine there is a decorated panel from the fourteenth century, called a rood screen. It is covered with carvings of Prince Brochwel on his horse, the huntsman with his horn, Saint Melangell, the hare and the dogs."

"Are there carvings of our ancestors, the cats?" I enquired.

"There are none of the cats, I'm afraid," she replied. "But cats prefer to remain unobserved, do they not?" I purred in agreement. "However," she continued, "Hopcyn is to be seen everywhere. He is in woodcarvings, stone carvings, sketches, paintings, and, what is more, his descendants still live in the area. Mind you, it's not to be wondered at. Saint Melangell is the patron saint of hares, you know."

"And of cats?"

"I expect so, although I'm not absolutely certain. But all kinds of animals and wildlife found sanctuary at Cwm

Wisdom

Pennant during Saint Melangell's life. In the wisdom given to her by the Holy Spirit she saw God's love in every creature and so the animals and wildlife came to her without fear because they knew that she was their friend."

"Thank you for relating the story to us," I said as I began to wash my paws. "Will another saint feature in the next heavenly manuscript?"

"Yes indeed. The next story will take us to Glendalough in Ireland where Saint Coemgen, better known as Saint Kevin, lived with yet more of your ancestors. He was born around the year 498 and died in 618, so he lived to the great age of one hundred and twenty. As cats never miss out on anything, your ancestors also lived remarkably long lives. By the end of that story we shall have traced your feline ancestry to Scotland, England, Wales and Ireland, in a circular tour, so to speak."

"How verrrry charming," I purred.

"A bird had settled on Coemgen's hand."

Chapter Four

Kindness
by Macushla of Gleann Da Loch

I am a long-haired cat of great age. My name is Macushla and I am mainly white, with a black patch above my left eye, and black along my tail and back – all of which is much admired. By human reckoning I am eleven years old, but I have heard it said that one year of a cat's life is equal to seven of a human's – therefore in cat years I am seventy-seven. The priest who lives with me is nearly eighty in human years. His name is Coemgen and we live in Gleann Da Loch, the Glen of Two Lakes, in Ireland. Coemgen is abbot of the monastery that he founded many years ago but he prefers to live as a hermit. You have probably never met a hermit. That's because hermits live by themselves in remote places. They do this so that they may be drawn closer to God. Not many humans understand why hermits go off and live in solitude but, of course, we cats understand − totally. For us, human company is good and has its place but we also need the freedom to be cats and to be alone.

Each year during Lent, Coemgen and I move out of the monastery. We go to live in a small dwelling, called a "hermitage" or "cell", by the side of the upper lake. It is shaped rather like a beehive and it is made of turf, stone and wattle (which is a woven lattice of wooden sticks). Further down the glen and beyond the lower lake are many more similar dwellings that are all part of the monastery. In these a monk lives alone but prays with the other monks and works with them in the fields or monastery. However, in two of these dwellings you will find not one but two occupants. The first is where Coemgen lives with me when we are not in the hermitage; the second is where a monk lives with

Kindness

another cat – Cadroe. Now Cadroe and I have been friends for more years than I care to remember. He is ten years old which makes him seventy in cat years. He has distinctive black stripes and patches, a white neck, white waistcoat and white paws. He, too, is much admired.

Having given you our ages, I would not be at all surprised if you dismissed us as too old to have adventures. But if you did that, you would be very much mistaken. I grant that we spend many hours asleep, but then you will understand, of course, that this is a habit we have cultivated since we were kittens, as all cats give priority to sleep, no matter what their age. Indeed, I would go so far as to say that long periods of sleep, the good air of the glen, and food provided at regular intervals by the monks who serve our needs, are undoubtedly the source not only of our longevity but also of our remarkable activity when we are awake.

The tales I am about to relate begin one spring day during Lent when Coemgen was living with me in our hermitage near the upper lake. Cadroe had travelled from his dwelling near the lower lake to spend some time with me, and our whole morning had been occupied with a mouse and a small shrew. The mouse eluded us, but the shrew finally admitted defeat and I promptly carried

The Cats' Family Tree

him off to the hermitage. There I deposited him on the floor where he remained, looking rather bewildered. As frequently happens on such occasions and always much to my annoyance, Coemgen came to the rescue of my prey and picked him up. But the shrew wriggled out of his hand, fell to the floor, and then ran up his leg. Now it was Coemgen's turn to wriggle – which he did as vigorously as his age would allow – with the result that the shrew once again fell to the floor. This time Coemgen grabbed him firmly, and without more ado carried him off to the bushes and released him.

Displeasure is a word that would not adequately describe my reaction. I sat and scowled until, with the stoicism that is peculiar to cats when faced with such a reversal of fortune, I ambled off. By now Cadroe had curled up and fallen asleep underneath a huge boulder near the shore of the lake. I decided to join him and within less than a minute I too was fast asleep. There we stayed in blissful slumber, so blissful that when we awoke the sun was setting over the lake.

I sat up, yawned, and then yawned again, blinked, and then closed my eyes as if to go back to sleep. But by now Cadroe was wide awake. "Look over there, Macushla," he said. "Isn't that Coemgen praying in the hollow of a

Kindness

tree? And look at those birds flying around the tree. Why, some of them are perching on his shoulders and on his outstretched hands!"

"So they are," I replied, all drowsiness vanishing instantly. "He often prays with his hands outstretched, but I've never seen birds perched on them before."

"Those birds are right-looking eejits," said Cadroe. "Birds should perch on trees, not on people. Surely they don't think that Coemgen is a branch of the tree?"

"I reckon that is what they think, Cadroe," I replied.

"Well then, they're certainly eejits," said Cadroe.

We sat and watched. Some of the birds began to preen themselves, others flapped their wings. Soon all had settled down for the night on Coemgen's shoulders and hands. But Coemgen did not move. He was deep in prayer.

"This is all very strange," observed Cadroe after we had watched for an hour or more. "But I for one have no intention of staying here for the rest of the night. I have things to do."

I followed him into the wood of ancient oaks. We spent the night mooching and prowling around but succeeded only in disturbing an odd duck or two dozing underneath the riverbank. With the coming of dawn we returned to our vantage point under the boulder. Coemgen was still kneeling in prayer with his arms outstretched, but all the birds had vanished – all, that is, except one. A bird had settled on Coemgen's hand and was busying herself as birds do when preparing a nest.

"Now, did you ever see anything like that?" I asked Cadroe.

"I never did," he replied. "I wouldn't be at all surprised if she laid an egg in his hand. C'mon on now. Let's go and investigate."

Creeping stealthily through the grass we reached a spot near to Coemgen and the bird and we crouched down behind a bush. Simultaneously, our hind legs moved from side to side and we swished our tails preparing ourselves to pounce. All at once the bird uttered a loud warble. "Hello," she said, cheerily. "I'm Bee the blackbird."

We sat up with a start. "Hello? What do you mean, 'hello'? Don't you realise that you are in danger?" I exclaimed. "Blackbirds don't warble and say 'hello' when they are in danger. My friend and I were just about to pounce on you."

Kindness

"Oh, I'm not in any danger," Bee replied. "Everyone knows that Coemgen is a holy man who protects birds and animals. That's why I've decided to make my nest in his hand. Look! He's even shaped his hand to accommodate me."

"Indeed, he has," Cadroe observed. "I've never seen anything like this. Ah, well now," he continued, addressing the bird. "I agree that Coemgen is a holy man, but are you not a bit of an eejit to be nesting in his hand? I mean, he won't be holding his hand up for ever, will he now?"

"Perhaps not," Bee replied. "But *I* am not the eejit, that's for sure."

"How so?" asked Cadroe.

"Well, from my bird's-eye view here on Coemgen's hand, I can see what you can't see."

"And what's that, may I ask?"

"A great cluster of nettles into which, had you been as foolish as to pounce on me, you would undoubtedly have fallen and stung yourselves."

"It's good of you to point that out," I said.

The Cats' Family Tree

"Not at all, don't mention it. Now, if you'll excuse me I'm about to lay an egg or two – an exercise that will call for a fair bit of concentration on my part."

"There!" said Cadroe. "What did I tell you? I knew she was getting ready to lay an egg. I've seen it happen before when I've been up a tree and spying on a nest."

"Lay an egg? You can't lay an egg on Coemgen's hand!" I exclaimed.

"Oh, can't I?" Bee retorted. "Just you wait and see."

There cannot be many people upon whose hands an egg is laid. But, as we watched, an egg was laid on Coemgen's hand by Bee the blackbird. Now, you may feel that by this time Coemgen had shown more than enough patience and hospitality to the blackbird. After all, his arms had been outstretched for all of the night and much of the day. But no, he kept his hand in the same position and, as you shall presently see, waited patiently until the young birds were fully hatched, and that, of course, took a very, very long time. Cadroe and I also waited patiently. The day after Bee the blackbird had taken up residence we returned to sit and "bird watch", so to speak. But "bird watching" can get monotonous and it was not long before we were totally fed up.

Kindness

"Is anything ever going to happen here?" I asked Bee the blackbird. "When is this egg going to hatch? Coemgen has eaten nothing since you first decided to make a nest of his hand and, what is more, neither have we."

"You should be grateful for the opportunity to fast, especially during this period of Lent," she replied, ruffling her feathers. "My presence here doesn't prevent you from finding food, does it? It's not as if I'm nesting on your paw, is it? I'm nesting in Coemgen's hand and he doesn't seem to mind – so why should you?" To which questions I could find no answers at all.

Now it so happened that a herd of cows was pasturing nearby. Cadroe and I were about to pad away from the scene when, all of a sudden, one of the cows left the herd and ambled over to Coemgen. The cow seemed vaguely familiar. It was only when she began to lick Coemgen's clothes that I remembered where I had seen her before.

"Are you not the cow that used to visit Coemgen years ago?" I asked.

"Sure, I'm the same cow," she replied.

"I'm probably having a 'senior moment'," I said, "but though your face is familiar and I remember that you

"I gave *the* best milk any cow had ever given."

used to visit Coemgen every day and lick his clothes, I'm sorry to say that I can't remember your name."

"I'm Ciara," she mooed.

"Of course you are. Now I remember. You used to leave the herd on their journey into the valley and make your way to Coemgen who was then living as a hermit in the hollow of a tree."

Kindness

"Sure, that's what I did," Ciara replied. "And as I remember, he was sharing the tree hollow with you at the time, was he not?"

"He was," I replied.

"Ah well, it's great to meet you again, after all these years."

"Excuse me," said Cadroe. "When you have completed all these pleasantries perhaps I could have a word?"

"Certainly," I said. "What is it you want to say?"

"May I ask where all this is leading? I mean, what has this cow licking Coemgen's clothes got to do with anything at all?"

"Well now," said Ciara the cow, "it's like this. When I visited Coemgen all those years ago I gave the best milk any cow had ever given and plenty of it. And that was all because I touched the clothes of this man of God."

"Ah, go away with you!" Cadroe retorted. "You don't expect me to believe that, do you?"

"Believe it or not," said Ciara. "It's the truth, sure it is. All the people in these parts know about it and I wouldn't

The Cats' Family Tree

be at all surprised, sure I wouldn't, if one day the story receives hagiographical recognition."

"Hagio... gra... what?" exclaimed Cadroe.

"She means," I explained, "that the story will be written in the lives of the saints."

"Oh will it now? Well, that will be a fine thing, sure it will, but it won't help Coemgen or Macushla here or me to get anything to eat, now will it?"

"I was coming to that very point," said Ciara. "When Coemgen lived in the tree hollow he used to gather herbs for his food. Now it so happens that in the course of my grazing excursions I have come across a particularly fine growth of herbs. From now on I shall carry a bunch of herbs in my mouth each day and bring them to Coemgen."

"Sure, that would be a fine thing too," I said.

And that is exactly what happened. Each day Ciara the cow came to Coemgen and fed him with herbs. When the young birds were hatched and ready to fly it was almost Easter and it was only then that Coemgen went back to his monastery to join his brother monks in celebrating the death and resurrection of the Lord.

Kindness

Another time, when we were all back living in the monastery, Cadroe and I returned to the monastery one day after exploring in the woods and found that a curious sight awaited us. In the corner of a room was what appeared to be a small bundle of clothes. From within this bundle there came a gurgling sound. Crouching low, we cautiously approached the bundle and then stopped short and sat up.

"Have you ever seen anything like that?" I said. "What is it?"

"'Tis a baby," Cadroe replied. "Have you never seen a baby before?"

"I never have," I said.

"All the monks here would have been babies once, you know."

"Would they now? Sure, I never knew that."

"But what is a baby doing here in the monastery?" he asked. "Babies aren't usually found in monasteries, as far as I know. Perhaps if we listen in on what the monks are talking about after supper we'll find out why the baby is here."

The Cats' Family Tree

And so that evening, when the monks were talking together during their weekly half-hour of conversation (they lived in silence at all other times), we trotted into the room, sat down by the fire, curled up, and then, looking as if we were asleep, listened to all they had to say. After a while we lay on our backs with our legs lifted high and basked in the fire's warm glow.

"Wouldn't it be just great to be a cat?" suggested one of the monks, Brother Ronan by name, as he observed our blissful state.

"Nothing to do but sleep well and go out whenever you want – sure 'tis a great life," said another, Brother Fintan.

How little they know, I thought to myself.

"The baby is sleeping well too," said Brother Ronan.

"What baby might that be?" Brother Fintan enquired.

"Why, the son of Colman, chief of northern Leinster. The baby's name is Faolain and his father has placed him in the care of Abbot Coemgen."

"Why ever would he do that?" asked Brother Fintan.

"Because," said Brother Ronan mysteriously, "his life is in mortal danger from witchcraft and Colman has asked

Kindness

Coemgen to protect him. The problem is," he continued, "the baby needs milk and the cows have gone to pastures many miles away in the mountains. Sure, Coemgen doesn't know what to do about it at all and he's praying to God for help."

Cadroe and I sat up together and looked hard at each other. Then we had a wash, as all cats do when contemplating the next course of action, after which we waited until the monks had filed silently out of the room. "Are you thinking what I'm thinking, Cadroe?" I asked.

"I don't know what you're thinking, sure I don't, but I'm thinking that Ciara the cow might provide the milk," he replied. "Is that what you're thinking?"

"It is what I'm thinking," I said. "And I'm also thinking that as Ciara used to leave the herd when she visited Coemgen she is obviously an independent sort of cow, so perhaps she has stayed behind and not gone off with the other cows."

"That's good thinking, Macushla, sure it is," said Cadroe. "We had best try and find her as soon as we can."

Early next morning we made for the tree hollow where we had last seen Ciara. But when we arrived she was not to be seen anywhere. Then from a branch of a tree came

The Cats' Family Tree

a familiar noise. "Hello," warbled Bee the blackbird. "I've brought my youngsters out for the day but they've started having tantrums so I've left them to fly around by themselves for a while. I mean, it's the best thing to do. You can't argue with them when they are having tantrums, can you?"

"Er… no," I replied. "But tell me, please, have you seen Ciara the cow?"

"You won't find Ciara around here now. She's gone off with the rest of the herd through the mountains. She didn't want to go, but the herdsman was quite insistent about it."

"Oh dear, what are we to do?" I exclaimed. Then I told Bee the blackbird our story and why we needed milk for the baby.

"I know a doe that lives near here. She might be able to help," she said. "Her name is Davnet. If you wish, I could fly around and look for her."

"Oh, would you?" I said eagerly. "And when you find her could you tell us where she is so that we can go and ask for her help?"

Kindness

"It will be a pleasure. I'm always willing to oblige," she warbled enthusiastically as she flew off.

Within a very short time Bee the blackbird was back. "I've found her!" she sang. "She's on the hill, near the top of the waterfall. If you go now you should see her."

Cadroe and I ran along the riverbank and then scooted up the side of the waterfall. We reached the top and there on the opposite side of the hill was a doe busily occupied in grazing.

"Are you Davnet?" I miaowed.

"Who wants to know?" was the reply.

"I'm Macushla and this is Cadroe," I said. "Forgive us for disturbing you, but have you got any milk?"

"So you've run out of milk, have you?" she replied. "Sorry, but I don't supply cats with milk. It's for deer."

"What did she say?" asked Cadroe. "She doesn't supply milk because it's too dear?"

"Please excuse my friend," I said to the doe. "He's getting a little hard of hearing. It's his age, you know." And then

115

The Cats' Family Tree

I added quickly, "I must explain that the milk is not for us, it's for a baby."

"For a baby, you say? Ah well now, that's different. Just tell me where the baby is and I'll supply the milk."

"The baby is living in the monastery and is under the care of Abbot Coemgen," Cadroe answered.

"Lead on!" exclaimed Davnet the doe. "Abbot Coemgen is the friend of all animals and birds and we would do anything to help our friend."

We led Davnet down the hillside and along the track to the monastery. From that time on until the baby was grown she came twice a day from her pasture to be milked by one of the monks. But neither Coemgen nor anyone else ever knew of what Cadroe and I had done – and that's as it should be. Every cat has a secret life known only to God who made us.

Kindness

Goldilocks sighed contentedly as she finished reading the manuscript to me. "Your ancestors and everyone else in the story were all very helpful. They seem to have cared about each other. I find this most encouraging."

"I'm so pleased that you do," I said. "We try to be helpful to the priest, you know."

"Do you indeed? In what way, may I ask?"

"Well, we feel at times that he needs exercise. He has given us a tunnel covered in cloth. It's a sort of plaything, I suppose. His idea is for us to run through the tunnel – which we do, of course. Like Bee the blackbird in the story, we are always willing to oblige. However, I prefer to run through it when he throws a small ball along the hallway of the house. I then chase after it and, if his aim is true, I kick the ball through the tunnel. Of course, it gives me exercise, but, more importantly, it gives him exercise as I demand that he throws the ball numerous times, otherwise I usually miaow strenuously."

"How very helpful of you," Goldilocks said. She sighed, raised her eyes heavenwards and yawned. It was pretty obvious that a ball and tunnel had failed to grab her enthusiasm. "May we move on?" she asked. "Perhaps you

The Cats' Family Tree

have a question arising from the story I have just read to you?"

"I have a question," said Ko-Ko. "I remember you told us that Coemgen was better known as Saint Kevin. My question is: why did Saint Kevin…"

Goldilocks interrupted him, "I am most impressed that you remember his other name. You have evidently been paying attention."

"One tries one's best," he replied, rather bashfully.

"Please do continue with your question."

"I was going to ask why Saint Kevin allowed Bee the blackbird to make a nest in his hand. Could he not have removed her from his hand and placed her in the tree?"

"An excellent question," Goldilocks said approvingly, "and I think the answer is that had he not allowed the blackbird to nest in his hand and therein to lay an egg we would have been deprived of Macushla's story, would we not?"

"I suppose that's true," he admitted.

"Moreover," Goldilocks continued, "many generations

Kindness

of pilgrims to Glendalough would also have been deprived of the story of Saint Kevin and the blackbird and of the many images of the saint with a bird in his hand – one of which is to be seen near to the ruins of the cell where he lived with Macushla. And that would have been most regrettable."

"I couldn't agree more," I said. "There would have been neither story to tell nor images to create."

"Exactly so – but I think the principal reason why Saint Kevin did not remove the blackbird from his hand was because he was at prayer. Do you recall your ancestor so rightly spoke of sleep as being an essential part of a cat's day?"

"Yes, I thought it was an astute observation. But what have a cat's sleeping habits to do with prayer?"

"Precisely this," she answered. "Whereas for a cat sleep is all-important, for Saint Kevin it was not sleep but prayer that was essential. In allowing the blackbird to nest in his hand and in showing her kindness his prayer was seen in action, and that is the meaning of true piety, one of the gifts of the Holy Spirit."

Curiously, as she finished speaking, a blackbird landed on her head, stayed awhile and then flew off. "I thought

The Cats' Family Tree

for a moment that history was about to be repeated," I said.

"I'm rather glad it wasn't," Goldilocks replied. "It would have totally ruined my hairstyle."

The next morning we trotted along to visit Goldilocks again. "Good morning, Goldilocks," I said. "I've come to see if you have another story for us."

"Very much so," she replied excitedly. "The angelic archivists delivered it by special delivery last night. I must say that the manuscript is quite extraordinary."

"Why is that?" I asked eagerly.

"Well, it seems that two of your ancestors were involved in the ministry of no less a person than Saint Francis of Assisi and that they had more than a nodding acquaintance with the Pope of that time, Honorius III."

"That has certainly made my day!" I purred.

"And mine!" cried Ko-Ko, with a piercing miaow.

"I expect it has," she said. "It means that, having visited places where saints lived with your ancestors in the first millennium, we are now going to be taken into the early

Kindness

part of the second millennium – to the year 1223, to be exact. It also means that we shall make a journey, in a manner of speaking, to Italy where all the following events took place."

"How verrrry enticing!" I exclaimed.

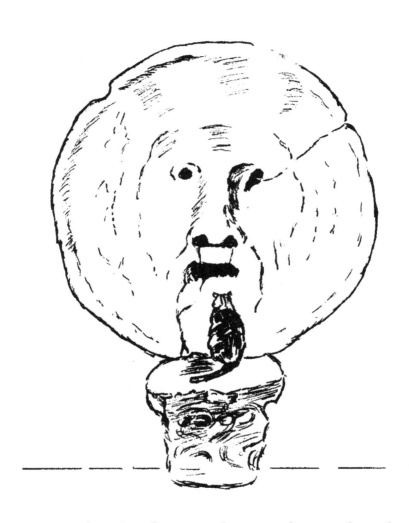

"I sat on the plinth ... and had profound thoughts."

Chapter Five

Perseverance
by Cocco of Greccio

My name is Cocco. I am a Church Cat and I live in the little village of Greccio that nestles in a valley not far from Assisi. What a lot of fuss and bother there has been in our village of late! Rumours fly here and there; people pretend to know nothing when they obviously know something; small groups huddle in corners and move off as soon

The Cats' Family Tree

as you approach. Even animals and birds do the same. Sheep gather together and look at you disdainfully as they trot off, other cats ignore you and geese attack you. It's all very odd.

Recently, I was talking to my friend, Saggio, about this state of affairs and he offered some good advice.

"It's like this," he said. "People around here know that something big is going to happen. Some know what it is, others pretend they know what it is, but no one wants anyone else to think that they don't know what it is. Of course, I know what it is, as I am an old and wise cat. If I tell you what it is, don't let anyone think you know. Pretend to know nothing."

"Thank you," I said. "I'll do as you say."

"*Prego*," he replied. "What's going to happen is this: Francis of Assisi is coming here at Christmas with his latest idea. He's arranged for what he calls a crib to be erected – it will be a scene just like the stable in which Jesus was born. Of course, the big question is: who is to be invited to this major event? It's causing a lot of ill feeling, I can tell you. Why, just listen to those two over there."

Perseverance

He directed my attention to a nearby field where an ass and a cow were complaining bitterly.

"After all," said Asfodelo the ass, "everyone knows there was an ass in the stable where Jesus was born, but I haven't been invited. I'm quite put out by it."

"So am I," agreed Margheritina the cow. "Cattle were there too, you know."

"How upsetting," I observed. "But tell me," I asked Saggio, "why have only some residents of our town been invited? Surely Francis would want all of us to be there?"

Saggio purred in agreement. "Of course he would. But he's not the one who decides, is he? Those in charge are the ones who decide and they want only a select number to be invited. It's all to do with 'cutbacks' and 'cost-effective strategies' – so I've heard."

"This cannot be right," I replied. "Jesus says that when we have a party we are to invite people who are poor, crippled, lame and blind. I would have thought that the same principle applies here. Is there no higher authority to whom we could appeal?"

Saggio stretched out his front paws and sat down. He said something but I couldn't quite make out what it

The Cats' Family Tree

was as he was licking his left front paw and then washing the back of his ears.

"I didn't quite catch that," I said. "Were you talking about 'soap' and 'fat'?"

"Not at all," he snapped. "I said that you could appeal to the Pope or have a word with his cat."

"The Pope or his cat?" I exclaimed. "How could I speak to the Pope or his cat?"

"You could go to Rome and ask to see them," he replied. "You can't expect me to travel that far as I am a senior cat, but you are a young cat and the exercise would do you good. In fact, as you are a Church Cat a pilgrimage to Rome would be most fitting."

"And how, may I ask, would I get to Rome? I don't know the way."

"All roads lead to Rome," he replied brightly. "So you can't go far wrong."

And so it was that I set off on my pilgrimage. Skirting the edge of the mountains, I travelled by night and slept most of the day until, after many weeks, I arrived in Rome.

Perseverance

How different it was from my native village! All hustle and bustle, and in all the ancient ruins – cats, hundreds of us! How was I to find the Pope's cat among so many? But I was determined to do so as I was sure his cat would help me to put my request before the Pope.

As I trotted along and mooched around, I asked other cats if they could help me. Some turned up their noses and walked away. Others stood their ground, tightened every sinew and growled at me. But of those who replied, none knew anything about the Pope's cat. By now, I was tired and hungry. An unattended tray of fish on a market stall, too tempting to resist, caught my attention. I jumped onto the stall, grabbed a fish and ran behind a pillar at the front of a nearby church. No one seemed to bother. They were all engaged in animated conversation. Having eaten my fill and had a wash, I decided it was time to sleep. I curled up in a corner near the pillar where I could remain unobserved. But I was awakened by a voice.

"*Buongiorno*! To whom have I the pleasure of speaking?"

The voice came from an enormous marble image. It was circular and fixed to the wall. It had eyes, a nose and a mouth that was permanently open.

The Cats' Family Tree

"I'm Cocco and I'm a Church Cat," I replied drowsily.

"Are you indeed? Well, I'm La Bocca della Verità otherwise known as 'The Mouth of Truth' – but you can call me 'Bocca'."

"Thank you. I will. But would you mind telling me where I am?"

"You are in the portico of the church of Santa Maria in Cosmedin. It's a very old church. But I am even older. I've been around here for centuries. I remember when there was a temple on this very spot. It was dedicated to the goddess Ceres. The ancient Romans believed that she gave special protection to the harvest and agriculture. As I am an image of Faunus, the Roman god of fields, herds and wildlife, it's rather appropriate that I'm here, don't you think?"

"I expect it is," I said, somewhat mystified.

"Of course, I've seen many changes over the years," Bocca continued. "Indeed, I remember when this part of Rome was a cattle and grain market. That was in the early days of the Roman Republic. Years later, food was organised and distributed from nearby to all the people

Perseverance

in Rome. I thought of that when you brought your stolen fish here."

"I'm sorry about that but I was very hungry."

"*Prego*," he replied. "But allow me to continue. In the sixth century a small church was built where the present church stands and this became a centre for the relief of poor people and pilgrims."

"I'm a pilgrim," I said.

"Are you really? How fascinating. I don't think I have ever met a pilgrim cat before," said Bocca.

"I've come to Rome to see the Pope or his cat," I explained. "Francis of Assisi is coming to my home village of Greccio to bless the crib at Christmas and only a certain number of people have been selected to be present. I want to ask the Pope to allow everyone in the village to be invited."

"What an excellent idea. I do hope you are successful in your request."

"Do you really mean that?" I asked. "I've been travelling for such a long time but now that I've arrived in Rome

The Cats' Family Tree

and find cats everywhere I'm beginning to wonder if I shall ever find the Pope's cat. In fact, I'm asking myself if this was such a good idea, after all."

"Of course it's a good idea," Bocca replied. "Remember, I am the Mouth of Truth. I would hardly say something I didn't mean, would I?"

"I suppose not. But tell me, why are you called the 'Mouth of Truth'?"

"To be honest – as I have to be, of course – it is not a name that I am particularly fond of. Having been fashioned in the image of Faunus, I much prefer his name. But what really hurts is when people say that originally I was no more than a cover, albeit a rather elaborate one, for a drain. I was never a cover for a drain."

"A drain?"

"Yes, a drain. Rather humiliating, isn't it? Being thought of as a cover for a drain?" (He gave a little sob and tears began to flow from his eyes.)

"Oh, there, there," I purred, soothingly. "Drains are very important, and therefore drain covers are very important too."

Perseverance

"How kind of you to say so."

"*Prego*," I replied. "But I still don't understand why you are called 'The Mouth of Truth'."

"Well, it's because of what the ancient Romans did: they used to put their right hands into my mouth when taking an oath."

"How curious. Why did they do that?" I asked.

"By putting their hands in my mouth they promised the god Faunus to speak the truth, or to keep a promise. That's how it all began. But many centuries later, I was used as a means of testing people to see if they were telling the truth. You see, if people were accused of doing wrong and if it was suspected that they weren't telling the truth about it, they had to put their right hands into my mouth. If they persisted in being untruthful then it was thought that I would crunch their fingers – a sort of 'number crunching' exercise, I suppose."

"And did you ever crunch their fingers?"

"Of course not. Only God knows the truth in a person's heart. Besides, I don't have the teeth for that sort of

The Cats' Family Tree

thing. But perhaps I should add," he continued, "that none of this applies to cats."

"Naturally," I replied. "Cats always tell the truth. How could we do otherwise?"

"Exactly so," said Bocca. "It's only humans who don't tell the truth. Most know the difference between truth and falsehood but," he added darkly, "some convince themselves that what they know to be false is true and others that what they know to be true is false. And then, of course, there are others who don't seem to know the difference at all."

Curiosity now got the better of me. In front of Bocca was a plinth. I jumped onto it, stood on my hind legs and gave him a penetrating stare. Then I sat on the plinth, crouched down and had profound thoughts.

"What are you thinking about, little one?" he asked.

"I'm pondering the meaning of truth," I replied. "When the ancient Romans swore to tell the truth or to keep a promise, they were making a commitment, were they not?"

"They most certainly were. Truth always involves a commitment."

Perseverance

"Well, I believe it is true that God wants everyone to celebrate the birth of Jesus when Francis blesses the crib and I must be true to the commitment I have made to my friend Saggio."

"Yes, indeed you must."

And so I stood on my hind legs again and put my front right paw into Bocca's mouth.

"There," said Bocca, "that was painless, wasn't it? God always comes to the help of those who make a commitment to what is true. The Holy Spirit gives them the gift of fortitude and this makes them faithful and spiritually strong, especially when things are difficult."

"You seem remarkably well informed," I said.

"When one has been in a church portico for as long as I have, then one tends to pick up these theological snippets from time to time."

"I know exactly what you mean," I said. "I too, through making frequent visits to our little church in Greccio, have gained a similar knowledge. Most of my time in church is spent asleep, of course, but I make a special effort to stay awake when the priest delivers his sermons – as does the congregation, but with varying degrees of success."

"No. I'm a pilgrim and I've come *to* see the Pope."

Perseverance

"I have nothing but admiration for you and the congregation," said Bocca.

I gave a purr of appreciation. "*Arrivederci*, Bocca," I said, "and *grazie tante*."

"*Prego. Arrivederci*, Cocco," the Mouth of Truth replied.

I set off again on my journey and arrived at the ruins of the Forum. There, reclining on a large foot – the remains of a great statue – was a domestic long hair cat, mainly white but with a black patch above her left eye and black along her back and tail.

"Hello," she said. "What's your name?"

"I'm Cocco and I am a Church Cat."

"I am Signorina Machiavetti," she replied. "By a strange coincidence, I too am a Church Cat. What are you doing here? Are you a tourist?"

"No. I'm a pilgrim and I've come to see the Pope – or his cat – and to ask a favour for our village." Then I told her all about the goings-on in Greccio and explained that I wanted to ask the Pope to allow all the village residents to be present when Francis of Assisi blessed the crib on Christmas night.

"I followed her along the narrow streets."

"Your request seems very reasonable," she said. "Follow me."

I followed her along the narrow streets until at length we arrived in front of an enormous basilica and palace, the like of which I had never seen. People were gathered everywhere.

Perseverance

"This is the first and the mother of all the churches in the city and in the world," declared Signorina Machiavetti. "It is known as Saint John Lateran."

"This mass of people milling around frightens me," I said nervously.

"Oh, it's always like this during the day," she replied cheerfully. "Keep close to me. I know my way in and out of here like the back of my paw."

We sped through the crowds and on entering a great palace we arrived at the foot of a staircase. We both stopped short in our tracks and then sat down and had a wash. This, of course, took a considerable time but, having finished, Signorina Machiavetti announced (rather in the manner of a tourist guide), "Many years ago this palace belonged to an ancient Roman family, by name Laterani. In the fourth century the Emperor Constantine gave it to Pope Melchiades. But the family's name survived. That is why the basilica is called Saint John Lateran. This is the Lateran Palace. By the way, do feel free to ask questions."

"Thank you," I said. "Why are people climbing the staircase on their knees?"

The Cats' Family Tree

"These are the Scala Santa, the Holy Stairs. Jesus climbed these stairs when he was arrested and taken before Pontius Pilate. They were brought here from Jerusalem by Saint Helena, the mother of the Emperor Constantine. The people climb on their knees to do penance for their sins."

"We have a staircase in the church house where I live in Greccio," I said. "I frequently sit on one of the top stairs and observe what's going on below. Sometimes I go to sleep on the stairs and find it most relaxing."

"How fascinating," she said and gave a wide yawn.

"Many are the times," I continued, "when, after being busily occupied for most of the night, I climb the stairs before dawn, go into the priest's room, and either sit at the side of his bed and miaow or attack his feet."

"Why on earth do you do that?" she asked.

"To wake him up so that he can give me my breakfast, of course."

"Of course – how foolish of me to miss the obvious."

"He invariably gets up," I continued, "and then we both go down the stairs. Naturally, I lead him down and, with my tail in the air, I tack from side to side, but sometimes

Perseverance

I roll down the stairs on my back. Then I lead him into the kitchen and he gives me my breakfast."

"You seem to have educated him well," she observed. "Bravo!"

"*Prego*. It's all a matter of having a clear policy of educational objectives and strategies, you know."

I looked again at the staircase and wondered where it led. "Are we going to climb it?" I asked.

"That is certainly my intention," she replied. "But there are too many people here now. In a few minutes it will be siesta time. All these people will then disappear, as if miraculously, and nothing will happen anywhere for hours. That will be our opportunity to climb the stairs."

"Shall we climb on our knees so as to do penance for our sins?" I asked.

"Don't be silly. Cats don't climb things on their knees and, what is more, cats don't sin. We do as God intends us to do. Sadly, the same cannot be said for humans. Humans know what is right and wrong but sometimes they deliberately choose to do what they know is wrong."

The Cats' Family Tree

When all the people had left, we climbed the stairs and, on reaching the top, I followed Signorina Machiavetti along a maze of corridors. No one attempted to stop us. On the contrary, doors were opened and we were ushered through. Eventually we entered a room in which a man was seated at a desk. "Signorina Machiavetti!" the man exclaimed. "There you are! I haven't seen you for hours."

"This is the Holy Father," she whispered.

"The Holy Father!" I exclaimed. "So you must be his cat?"

"Obviously," she said with a rather superior air. "Now go and tell him why you are here."

Tell him? How was I to tell him? I sat and stared hard at him. The Holy Father stretched out his hand towards me, smiled and stroked me.

"I know what I'll do," I said to myself. "I'll do what all cats do when they want to show love or tell people something. I'll wrap myself around his legs and purr." And that is what I did.

"Ah, *piccino*! Have food, milk and whatever you need," he said kindly, and with that he blessed me.

"You are welcome to stay here for as long as you wish,"

Perseverance

said Signorina Machiavetti. "The accommodation is excellent and the food is second to none. I think you will find that, by coming here, you have well and truly landed on your paws."

"That is very gracious of you," I replied, "but I really must get back to Greccio before Christmas. I want to be there when Brother Francis blesses the crib. But first I must put my request before the Holy Father."

"In that case, this is what I suggest you do," she said. "Over the next few days you should acquaint yourself with the Holy Father's lap. I usually curl up on his lap when he is working at his desk. I am more than pleased for you to occupy that position – but only as a temporary arrangement, you understand."

"I would not wish for a moment to encroach upon your proper place," I said.

"*Prego*," she replied. "Now, the object of the exercise is this: Francis of Assisi will undoubtedly seek the Pope's consent to the erection of the crib at Greccio. As Christmas always seems to get earlier these days, I am sure that his request will arrive here very soon."

"Forgive me," I said, somewhat perplexed, "but what am

The Cats' Family Tree

I to do when the Pope receives this request? And what of my own request? How can I put that before him?"

"Oh, don't worry about any of that," she said. "Cast all your cares on the Lord and he will look after you."

The following day I jumped onto the Pope's lap as he sat at his desk. The next morning, when he was in his private chapel and meditating after celebrating Mass, I sat on his lap again. These exercises were repeated several times for almost a week until one morning, while the Holy Father was at his desk and I was asleep on his lap, his secretary entered the room.

"Holy Father, Brother Francis of Assisi has requested Your Holiness to allow a crib to be erected at Greccio this Christmas. He says that he wants to represent, as far as he can, how the Lord Jesus was born into poverty, laid on straw in a manger, with an ox and an ass for his companions."

At these words I awoke with a start and began to purr.

"Of course a crib may be erected," said the Holy Father. "Tell Brother Francis that I hope all the people of Greccio will be invited to its opening. Do you not agree,

Perseverance

piccino?" he said as he tickled me under my chin. My purrs grew louder.

I jumped off his lap. The Holy Father and his secretary left the room and I darted across to Signorina Machiavetti, bouncing sideways with my back arched – as I often do when in an exuberant mood.

"Did you hear that?" I exclaimed.

"I certainly did," she purred. "The Holy Father even asked your opinion on the matter. What more could any cat ask for?"

"What more, indeed?" I replied. "*Grazie tante.*"

"*Prego,*" she said.

After a day or two I set off on my journey back to Greccio where I arrived on Christmas Eve, just in time for the opening of the crib. A thin layer of snow was on the ground and on a hillside a stable had been built. Francis of Assisi had asked one of his friars to prepare the stable and to bring in real animals and to have a real manger with real straw so that everyone could see what it was really like when Jesus was born. Inside the stable were my friends, Asfodelo and Margheritina and, of course,

The Cats' Family Tree

Saggio, who, having heard that real animals were going to be there, had come along too. People had gathered all around and were holding candles and torches. Francis had brought together the whole village to give praise and thanks for the birth of Jesus, the Son of God!

And so ends the story of my pilgrimage to Rome, written at my dictation by the priest who lives with me in Greccio. Lest anyone should doubt its authenticity, I direct the reader to the Basilica di Porta Maggiore built by the ancient Romans. There you will see a beautiful stucco relief of two cats in ancient Greece. If they came to Rome all those centuries ago (as they obviously did) then need I say more?

"The Recording Angels tell me that this is the last of the heavenly manuscripts, at least for the present," said Goldilocks. "It's rather a pity, but there we are. If they find any more then of course I shall let you know immediately."

I was about to thank her when all at once I heard a sound. Ko-Ko and I turned our heads in the direction

Perseverance

of the sound but kept the rest of our bodies facing in the same direction as before. (It's a movement that owls do quite well, though obviously not as well as cats.) The sound was of the front door of the house being opened by the priest. He was wearing gardening clothes. As he walked down the path he spotted us.

"Hello, Mac. Hello, Ko-Ko," he said. "Do you want to go for a walk before I start working in the garden?"

I turned my head back towards Goldilocks. "Would you think us awfully rude if we joined him?" I asked. "He knows we always seize the opportunity to walk with him along the side of the beck."

"Not at all," she replied. "Do as your fancy takes you, by all means. It will give me an opportunity to catch up on my siesta. All this reading has rather interfered with my normal schedule, you know."

We scampered down the stone steps leading from the front door and, with our tails in the air, went ahead of the priest to the bottom of the garden where we patiently waited for him to open the gate. This he dutifully did and, following our usual custom, Ko-Ko trotted over to examine the inside of a water pipe that opens onto the beck and I stepped onto the stones at the water's

"Do you want to go for a walk before I start working in the garden?"

Perseverance

edge and had a drink. Then together we crouched at the edge of the bank and meditated on our next move, after which we padded slowly along until, with great spurts, we leaped over boulders, stones and tree roots exposed at the water's edge, overtook the priest, and dived into a clump of long grass. As we did so, there was a mighty screech and a pheasant flew out of the grass while at the same time a rabbit emerged, bounded along by the side of a drystone wall and then disappeared underneath a gorse bush. Naturally, we gave chase immediately but in spite of all our efforts the rabbit was nowhere to be seen and so we scampered up a tree almost to the top. By now the priest was underneath the tree.

"Mac! Ko-Ko! What are you doing up there? Do be careful. That branch looks very precarious."

How very silly, we thought. Does he not realise that we cats are as at home in trees as we are on the ground and that we know exactly what branches will or will not take our weight? We decided to ignore him.

"Well, if you are going to stay up there, I'm going back to the garden. I've got work to do," said the priest – and off he went.

The Cats' Family Tree

We sat in the tree for a long time and observed all that was going on. Then we decided to climb down and mooch around. All at once I spotted the rabbit bobbing through the grass and moving in the direction of the garden. The chase was on again! This time I caught him, carried him in my mouth across the garden, up the wooden steps to the back of the house, through the cat flap, into the house where – and I'm rather ashamed to admit this – the rabbit wriggled free and ran underneath a bookcase. I must have spent a full hour waiting for him to emerge – but he didn't. Eventually, I sat up, stretched out my front paws, had a wash and then ambled back into the garden.

By now Ko-Ko had joined the priest who, ignorant of all that had been going on, was happily engaged in sweeping leaves and twigs into a sack which he then took down to a large pile by the edge of the beck. Whenever he does this Ko-Ko finds it irresistible to pounce on the sack and sit on it while the priest drags it along. I joined in this exercise but only for a short time as this sort of thing can become rather boring after a while.

Ko-Ko and I decided to trot back to Goldilocks and resume our conversation. But when we arrived in the cemetery she was still asleep. I miaowed, Ko-Ko miaowed,

Perseverance

and together we miaowed again, but she did not stir. This was most inconvenient as we wanted to have some more conversation with her about our ancestors in Assisi and Rome. However, with all our activities even we were feeling drowsy. We decided to go into the house and have a sleep on our respective chairs.

When I woke up it was late evening. A noise made me sit up. I jumped off the chair to investigate. Ko-Ko did the same. The priest, who had been sitting on his chair, joined us and together we all crouched down and peered underneath the bookcase.

"It's a baby rabbit!" exclaimed the priest. "How long have you been there?" he asked the rabbit. "Did you bring him in, Ko-Ko? Or was it you, Mac?"

Well really! What a question! Obviously, he didn't come in by himself.

"Come on, little rabbit," said the priest. "Let me rescue you and take you out."

Not if I can help it, I thought. The priest reached under the bookcase and attempted to get hold of the rabbit but he couldn't stretch his hand far enough. I moved from one side of the bookcase to the other and then back again.

The Cats' Family Tree

Ko-Ko moved in the opposite direction, jumping onto the priest's back in the process. But the rabbit eluded cats and priest, scurried from his refuge, scampered across the room, and dived behind a magazine rack in the corner. Immediately the priest grabbed him and carried him off into the wood.

Frustrated by all of these goings-on, Ko-Ko and I decided to go into the church. First I and then Ko-Ko had a drink from the holy water stoup. The water was cool and refreshing and after we drank our fill, we had a wash, and settled down to sleep again.

"*Buona sera*, Signorina Macavity! *Buona sera*, Signor Ko-Ko!" said Saint Francis from his plinth near the organ. "*Come sta*? How are you?"

"Very well, thank you," I replied, "though I must say that I am in rather a huff." And I told him all about the rabbit.

"That is indeed frustrating," agreed Saint Francis, kindly. "But just think," he continued, "the rabbit is now restored to his family and friends, and so he must be very happy."

"Yes, I suppose so, if you look at it that way," said Ko-Ko. "My ancestor, Cocco, was very happy when he returned

Perseverance

to his friends after his pilgrimage to Rome. Goldilocks has been telling us all about it."

"Cocco? Not the Cocco who lived in Greccio?" exclaimed Saint Francis.

"The same," he said.

"Why, I knew him very well. He figured prominently when I blessed the crib at Greccio. And so he was your ancestor, was he? *Che meraviglioso!* How wonderful!"

"Yes, it is," I purred. "And what is more, he met my ancestor, Signorina Machiavetti, in Rome. She was the Papal Cat, you know, and she introduced him to the Pope."

"*Che fortuna!*" Saint Francis responded. "What a fortunate meeting!"

"Yes, it was indeed," I said, continuing to purr contentedly.

Perhaps that would have been the end of the matter had it not been for Saint Hubert. "Forgive me," he said, "I could not help but overhear your conversation. I would be most interested to know the full story of this pilgrimage to Rome and I am sure that I also speak for Saint Francis, do I not?"

The Cats' Family Tree

"*Certamente*," Saint Francis affirmed. "You certainly do. Would you be so kind as to tell us all about it?"

And so I told them the story just as Goldilocks had related it.

"It seems to me," said Saint Hubert when I had finished telling the tale, "that the illustrious ancestors of Ko-Ko and yourself are quite exemplary."

"*D'accordo,*" said Saint Francis. "Indeed, I couldn't agree more."

"How very kind of you to say so," I replied as once again I engaged in a continuous and now much louder purr.

"Don't mention it," said Saint Hubert.

"*Prego*," said Saint Francis.

"You see," explained Saint Hubert, "Cocco did not know how he would get to Rome or what difficulties he would meet on the way but he persevered with great fortitude. And Signorina Machiavetti was kindness itself. She helped Cocco to put his request to the Pope, and she was a true friend. I must say, I think they give a lesson to everyone on how to live under the guidance of the Holy Spirit."

Perseverance

By now Ko-Ko had joined me in purring and our purrs had grown very loud.

"Excuse me," said a voice from the apse of the church. It was Egremont the eagle. "Some of us are trying to sleep, you know."

"I do apologise," I said, "but we can't contain our happiness. That is why our purrs are growing louder by the minute."

"May we ask the cause of this strange phenomenon?" enquired Oxymoron the ox.

"Yes, do tell us," said Leonidas the lion. "We have all been woken up. Unless I have been roaring in my sleep… Have I been roaring in my sleep?" he asked the others. They shook their heads. "Well then, it must be your purrs that have woken us up and that is very strange, very strange indeed."

It was Kettledrum's turn to speak. "Your purrs have not woken me up, Miss Mac and Ko-Ko. I have been listening to what you have been saying to Saint Hubert and Saint Francis. I am so pleased that you have found out about your ancestors in Italy. Tell me, did you discover any more ancestors?"

The Cats' Family Tree

"Oh yes, we did," I replied excitedly, and Ko-Ko and I told Kettledrum and the others of how Goldilocks, with the help of the angelic archivists, had discovered that our ancestors were all Church Cats and had been friends of saints who loved animals and that our ancestors had dictated their autobiographical memoirs to scribes, and then I told their tales just as Goldilocks had related them to me, and I have related them to you, and then… and then, well, then we found that everyone in the apse had gone back to sleep. Even Saint Hubert and Saint Francis had gone to sleep. And we knew that Goldilocks had long since gone to sleep. So we decided it was again time for us to go to sleep.

We curled up at the foot of the altar steps and together purred a prrrrayer (only this time very quietly), as we thanked the Lord for our family tree.

"We decided it was again time for us to go to sleep"